Dilemmas in Classroom Assessment

Dilemmas in Classroom Assessment

AND WHAT TO DO ABOUT THEM

Portage & Main Press

EDITED BY ROBERT J. WILSON

Portage & Main Press acknowledges the financial support of the Government of Canada through the Book Publishing Industry Development Program (BPIDP) for our publishing activities.

Book and cover design: Relish Design Studio Ltd.
Printed and bound in Canada by Friesens

05 06 07 08 09 5 4 3 2 1

Library and Archives Canada Cataloguing in Publication

Dilemmas in classroom assessment: and what to do about them / edited by Robert J. Wilson.

Includes bibliographical references.
ISBN 1-55379-061-8

1. Students--Rating of. 2. Grading and marking (Students). 3. Educational tests and measurements. I. Wilson, Robert J., 1938-
LB3051.D54 2005 371.27 C2005-904755-0

PORTAGE & MAIN PRESS

100 – 318 McDermot Ave.
Winnipeg, MB Canada R3A 0A2
Email: books@portageandmainpress.com
Tel: 204-987-3500
Toll-free fax: 1-866-734-8477
Toll-free: 1-800-667-9673

Contents

Introduction

ROBERT J. WILSON

Assessment concerns everyone in education. Students learn early to take it seriously, more so as they pass through the system. Parents want to know how their children are doing, not only what they are learning but also how that learning compares to that of other children. Districts and provinces mandate assessments at all levels of the school system for purposes of accountability and program improvement. Even the country has assessment programs. Teachers and principals often feel great pressure to accommodate these levels of assessment requirements and, further, to try to sort out what makes the most educational sense to them. Our overall goal in this volume is to share what we have found that might help with some of the dilemmas this expansion of assessment creates.

First of all, some background. All the essays included here assume the same point of reference toward learning: the assessment information that benefits teachers most is information about growth in student learning. And good teachers show a willingness to transfer a great deal of the assessment process to students, no matter how young they may be. We believe that reliance on self-assessment and growth points the way to the resolution of many of the dilemmas that teachers face.

In a previous volume, Sue Fostaty Young and Robert Wilson (*Assessment and Learning: The ICE Approach*) produced a portable model of assessing growth and showed how teachers and students of all ages used it to facilitate student learning: the ICE model. The ICE model is not tied to any particular form of assessment (such as rubrics, assignments, or tests) but works with all of them. Nor does it depend on the teacher to be the monitor of learning unless needed or desired. Rather, it is most useful when it is taught to learners, even very young learners, so that they can identify where they are in their learning and will be able then to plot their own next steps.

Simply put, the ICE model holds that learning a new concept, a new attitude, or a new skill begins with discrete bits of knowledge. When you are presented with your first digital camera, for example, you begin by trying to discover what each icon means, what all the buttons do, and how the viewfinder works. You may follow the manual point by point to learn how to replace the batteries and how to use the on-screen menu, clicking through one line at a time. These basic learnings are called Ideas in the ICE model and are seen as essential building blocks to all learning.

The required steps become automatic as you play with the camera, and slowly you will discover shortcuts to the step-by-step approach. Combining a timed shot with a dark background becomes possible, and so will overlaying one image on another, for example. This linking of discrete pieces of knowledge occurs almost naturally as we learn, unless we are content with the more routine ways of doing things. In the ICE model, these linkages are called Connections. A variation of this form of connection occurs when you attach old learning (what you remember from your old camera that might still apply) with the new.

Finally, it may happen that your interest in the camera and what it can do moves into a desire to produce your own prints and using them to make cards and invitations. This inclination to take old learning and turn it in a new direction is characteristic of those who are motivated to take their learning deeper. We often see these novel elaborations happen in a hobby, a sport, or in the arts, but they can be encouraged in the school setting as well. In the ICE model, these elaborations are called Extensions.

One central dilemma in current classroom assessment is inherent in balancing both the kinds of assessments that help teachers and learners progress in the classroom and those that are required for evaluation purposes from outside the classroom. These external assessments are inevitably norm- or criterion-referenced (they compare student achievement to others, to the norm, or to some set of standards or outcomes, the criterion, or do both). The results from these external assessments can be useful to teachers (as several essays in this book make clear), but, if these types of data are the only ones that teachers have or create, then assessment will be less than helpful.

One aid has been particularly helpful to teachers and administrators who are wrestling with multiple and seemingly conflicting demands: collaboration. Many of the essays in this book illustrate how educators, when they work together, are able to capitalize on their discrete understandings in ways that further their collective enterprise. When schools are more than collections of individuals, and when they capitalize on the relationships that blossom there, they succeed in using assessment information in positive ways.

HOW THE CHAPTERS ARE ORGANIZED

To make the information in this volume accessible, each contributor has followed the same format. Each briefly describes a scenario that illustrates a current issue. A summary of key points in the essay follows, and the bulk of the chapter contains jargon-free information and advice on how the dilemma can be solved, with lots of examples. Where technical terms are used, a definition follows within the body of the text.

HOW THE BOOK IS ORGANIZED

If your interests are primarily in classroom practices, look to the first essays in Section I for a source of practical ideas. If you are interested in school-level practice, look at Section II for ideas about creating an environment where individuals, working together, can provide a powerful context for improved practices. Finally, if you are dealing with externally produced assessments (a newer challenge for practising educators), look at Section III for ideas to help use external assessments purposefully while minimizing negative effects.

Within each section, the chapters are organized from specific to general, and from practical to theoretical. In Section I, "Classroom Practices," for example, David Notman gives a clear step-by-step method of involving students and their parents in the assessment process. Later on, John O. Anderson describes the criteria generally needed to ensure good assessment no matter how it is conducted.

The authors of the essays are a varied lot. Some are classroom teachers, and all have taught extensively at some level in the educational system. Some have been administrators. Others have spent considerable time studying assessment issues formally in graduate programs. Almost all have worked intimately with the others over a sustained number of years to hone the insights you will find in their essays. Some suggested readings are provided at the end of the volume.

We want to have the uses of assessment for positive educational purposes dominate the discussion. This outcome can occur only if we all understand what assessment is (and is not) and work to have its strengths rule. We hope this volume provides just such a background for you and your colleagues.

I Classroom Practices

The first six essays in this section are written by practising teachers; they write about how they have learned to handle certain enduring challenges in classroom assessment. How, for example, can a teacher do all that marking? How can a teacher assess very young children in ways that help them learn? What kinds of assessment practices would help low-achievers and exceptional students track their own progress but not see it as a lesser accomplishment than that of other students? How can teachers help parents wanting to work with their children at home?

The last four chapters look at classroom issues more generally. The emphasis is on techniques for making and recognizing reliable and valid assessments, for understanding the differences between quantity and quality in learning, and appreciating what distinguishes "subjective" from "objective" in the context of a teacher's practice. The section ends with an examination of the link between current notions of what learning is and how these fit with current approaches to assessment.

Moving from Marking to Assessing

1

DAVID NOTMAN

SCENARIO

Virginia hated marking essays. Here it was, Saturday night, all her friends were going to see the opening of *Fiddler on the Roof*, the annual musical put on by the local theatre company. And here she was, marking essays—thirty-four of them. It would be a little more palatable to her if she thought that her marking of the essays would have any lasting influence on the students who had written them. But she didn't believe that at all. So she was missing a special Saturday night out, bored out of her mind, and all for nothing.

She had reached Damien's paper: no thesis statement of any note, a short, quick attempt to say something he thought was relevant, or at least thought that the teacher would think was relevant, a couple of quotes, badly footnoted, and a facile conclusion. Virginia wrote a large *D* on the bottom of the last page and made extra comments to summarize the lengthy notes she had already included in the margins. "What's the point?" she thought. "I'm sure Damien is making the same mistakes on this essay as he has made on all the essays he has written since Grade 9." For a brief moment, it occurred to her to look up all the past grades for each of the student's papers she had left to mark and just write that mark down on the bottom of their essays. She was sure no one would care or even notice. "Why am I marking these things in the first place?" she moaned.

WHAT YOU WILL LEARN IN THIS ESSAY

- how to make the assessment process useful for both you and your students;
- how to involve parents in the process, which can be both helpful and exhilarating;
- how to mark less and enjoy assessment more.

DISCUSSION

Assessment as Grading

Virginia doesn't hate assessment, nor does she think evaluating students is pointless. She appreciates the fact that students need feedback to measure their personal growth and that she, as the teacher, needs to know the progress of each individual in her care.

What she does hate, however, is assigning a letter grade or a numeric grade to a piece of student work. She feels as though all she is doing is setting up a series of obstacles for her students in the form of assignments and test questions; the students who get through the obstacle course win. But she is the only one who knows the course, the only one who sets up the barriers. She can make the jumps straightforward or hide them to surprise the competitors. Even though all the students start at the same place, she designs the course so that very few of the starters can finish in first place.

So why does Virginia assign marks? The first reason has to do with the school's rules; her school expects her to submit marks for the report cards and student records that, by law, are required. The school uses these marks to calculate averages and award subject prizes and scholarships. Marks are the only criteria that most schools use to rank their students, and ranking students is standard policy in most schools.

Parents ask for marks and feel that marks indicate the level of success in school. This makes sense to them partly because they themselves received marks in school and they know how different an 87 is from a 42. The parents of high-achieving students feel that there is a difference between an average grade and the one their child receives. Too, they feel that a mark reflects the degree to which the student has mastered the course material, although they very likely don't know what constitutes that course material. They accept the marks on a report card as an act of faith that their child has been assessed fairly.

Many students, too, are motivated by marks; they use them as a reflection of personal worth. These same students spend much of their day attempting to master and memorize large chunks of material that will help them get a 95, help them get a scholarship, help them feel a high level of self-esteem. The praise lavished on the student with high marks at recognition assemblies, during graduation ceremonies, and on honour rolls provides students with a way of achieving recognition outside the gym, playing field, bandstand, or stage.

But do students really want marks to measure their learning? Do they see their marks as a reflection of what they now know that they didn't know before, or do they see their marks as a completion of a goal; another assignment finished, test written, essay done. Has their focus been on the tool used to mark them or on the learning that the tool is meant to measure? Virginia is beginning to think her students are focussed on the tools.

Virginia also feels that she is locked into a system that is perpetuated historically rather than logically, and that few of her colleagues actually think about marking but do it because everyone else does it. They set tests, assign essays, and give homework as a tradition that is unrelated to actual learning but designed to perpetuate "school" as a social institution. It has been ever thus for teachers, students, their parents, and their grandparents before them. Even the testing process has its ceremonies and rituals: the room set up in precise, numbered rows, patrolled by tissue- and foolscap-wielding teachers in soft-soled shoes, the rules of entry and departure concerning the precise amount of time students must remain in the room, how to request bathroom privileges, and where to put backpacks and books. The students' desks are festooned with lucky amulets, and exam monitors enforce strict silence as they patrol in ceaseless rounds. There is no place on earth that this represents. It is only the created reality of the exam room.

And our post-secondary institutions maintain the same traditions, for the same reasons. The rules are institutional. Colleges and universities use marks to determine whom they let in and whom they exclude. Although some programs ask for anecdotal comments, letters, and portfolios, most schools still rely on marks, placing a major obstacle in the way of any high school that might want to change its marking traditions.

Assessment as Part of Learning

Virginia was thinking about her workload recently over a quiet coffee in a local bookstore. She was distracted slightly by thoughts about how much time she had left on her parking meter. "I should have taken a cab or, better still, the bus," she thought. She felt a brief moment of guilt as she pictured her bike gathering dust in the garage. "Oh well, at least I'm here and can take a few minutes for myself. I guess it really doesn't matter how I got here." And that's when she had her assessment epiphany!

The bookstore visit was her specific objective for that day. She was in the bookstore and had therefore achieved her objective. Did it matter what method she had used to get here? Only if her specific objective was to experience a bus ride, or negotiate a parking lot, or learn the procedure for using a cab. "Too often," she thought, "I'm grading process, not product."

When we set tasks for students that incorporate a number of expectations or objectives, we can measure the degree of success they have in meeting all of them by determining how well they performed the task. Let's assume that a course in urban environments required that, by the end of the course, the student would be able to: (1) take public transit to a specific location; (2) visit the specific location; and, (3) take a taxi home from the specific location. The student returns to class with three artefacts: (1) a bus transfer receipt with the time printed on it; (2) a receipt from a purchase made that day at the featured location; and (3) a dated receipt from the cab. Is there any doubt that the student has met all three expectations?

Teachers could use tests, essays, quizzes, or any other evaluation method to determine whether each student possessed the skills necessary to make this trip. But these tests, essays, and quizzes are not the kind that need to be marked. They are only signposts along the path to the fundamental task that the student will perform. What the student's performance on this kind of test indicates is what he or she still needs to learn.

Each expectation in a course will include one or more tasks that students could perform to illustrate understanding of the material. The teacher's role is to determine what these tasks should be and combine them, if possible, into a larger project. The teacher could even involve the students themselves in producing (and therefore owning) the assessments. Once Virginia began the process of converting her course expectations into a series of practical, interesting tasks, she began to notice something: her course became more relevant to her and, more importantly, to her students. She was beginning to see interconnections in the course material that she had never noticed before, as several tasks were combined into meaningful projects.

Portfolios

A portfolio, conceived of as a series of interrelated tasks performed by a student, is useful for all concerned. Each piece of the portfolio relates, in some way, to every other piece, and, when the student draws all the pieces together, the portfolio is finished. The teachers can use the portfolio to help determine the student's progress or, if it is required, the student's grade.

The work represented in a student's portfolio may vary in the level of quality from that of the other students. Virginia knows that some students will write a better movie review than other students will, for example, or a student's movie review may not be as well written as his or her sports commentary. The course expectation states that, by the end of the course, a student should be familiar with various writing formats, including movie reviews. Virginia realizes that, if a student can write a movie review, he or she will have become familiar with the movie-review type of writing. This is Virginia's interpretation of the expectation. She knows that, when one student writes a better movie review than another student, the quality factor should be rewarded. A great movie review will receive a better mark than a standard one.

When Virginia teaches how to write movie reviews, she has her students develop a movie-review template, which includes all the features that a standard, professionally written, movie review contains, such as the name of the film, the actors in it, a brief plot summary that does not reveal the ending, and a statement about how the reviewer feels about the movie that indicates whether it is recommended. Virginia marks all the students' movie reviews at the same time. She begins by collecting the rough drafts, which she returns with corrections and suggestions for improvement. (She is quite happy teaching students to write movie reviews, even though it takes a long time to assess, because she gets to know a lot more about movies that she doesn't have time to see!)

Virginia's epiphany in the coffee shop has caused her to examine her assumptions, and her teaching of movie reviews changes dramatically. For example, the course expectation does not require or state, anywhere, that students need to write a movie review. Nor does it suggest that what students write be well-written. Her lesson on the movie review certainly demonstrates the style of the movie review. But Virginia is now asking herself, "How would I know that a student understands the format of a movie review? What could a student do to illustrate his or her familiarity with that type of writing?"

Virginia can think of many ways. Students might collect a few movie reviews and determine how closely they conform to the template discussed in class. They might compare written movie reviews with radio or television reviews. They might analyze the style of two different reviewers. Or they might write their own reviews. As long as the student can demonstrate that he or she is familiar with a specific type of writing (in this case movie reviews), then the student has fulfilled the course expectation.

The student could be responsible for selecting how this expectation would be met and submit the "proof" into the portfolio. Throughout the term, the student could return to the work, make corrections, have others comment on it, or add more information. Virginia dips into the portfolios regularly, armed with a checklist, to keep students on track. She makes suggestions, provides assistance, directs the student to various resources, and scaffolds the work in other ways, but the movie review assignment does not get marked. It is simply included.

For expectations where there is a clear quality component, such as, for example, "Students will be able to compose a letter of application that will make a positive impression on a prospective employer," the quality of the letter should be graded. But Virginia herself does not need to do the grading. The expectation dictates the assignment and provides a method by which it can be assessed: Does the letter make a positive impression on a prospective employer? Local human resources employees could be co-opted into acting as judges of the letters on a scale, as long as each of the assessors had the same scale, such as a simple checklist. Once students received the letter and the assessment, they would include it in their portfolio. At any time, any student could attempt to improve his or her submissions.

Conferencing

The portfolio is complete when all of the requisite parts have been placed in it. The student uses the parts to create a whole, and the whole becomes the main artefact for assessment. Students can turn their portfolios in to the teacher, who will mark them, but as each component piece probably requires some explanation, it makes more sense (and is a lot more fun) if the student chooses to engage in conferencing. Conferencing provides an opportunity for students to express themselves and demonstrate their knowledge to others. These others might be the teacher, other students, their parents, or members of the community. If appropriate technology were available, conferencing could occur on the Internet, and students could have international others for their conferences.

Student-Parent Conferencing

Virginia arranged for the students in one of her English classes to conduct conferences with one parent (or both if they were available). The students wrote invitations to the people they wished to have attend, and included one of their favourite poems. The invitations stated that the students would appreciate the opportunity to present selected pieces as works in progress contained in their portfolios. Each invitee was asked to act as both an audience and a sounding board as the students described their work. As well, each invitee was asked to be an informal evaluator of the course and the student's progress in it. Virginia set aside three late afternoons and evenings for the conferences, and she organized the classroom so that at least three conferences could occur at once; she felt that parents and students alike might be more relaxed if there were several conferences happening at the same time. (She had noticed that most parents entered the classroom tentatively, as if they were entering alien and slightly frightening territory.)

The portfolios consisted of examples of various types of writing: some that the students had done themselves, some that they had found and critiqued, and some that other students had done that they particularly liked. Students were to discuss with their guests the reasons for their choices. Each conference was scheduled to last twenty minutes. Virginia's primary reason for hosting the conferences was to provide parents with information about their children's progress in the course. The portfolio would not be officially graded until the course ended, so parents needed some current feedback, and Virginia felt that they could learn more from an interview than from a report card. After they were over, she discovered several more good reasons to have conferences.

Virginia was not part of the conferences themselves; she performed the roles of official greeter, problem-solver, and summarizer. The students conducted the interviews, and the first thing Virginia noticed was how enthusiastically the students took over. The classroom was now their territory, and their parents were their guests. She also noticed that many students clutched their portfolios tightly, as if to say, "This is mine. You will see it when I'm ready." Then the magic happened. Students let loose. They talked, laughed, discussed, questioned, and confidently showed their stuff. This was their work, their effort, and their moment. This was what they knew. They owned this material and they were confident about it. There wasn't a question they couldn't answer or a piece of work that was not part of them. Virginia was amazed. The parents were amazed. The interviews lasted a lot longer than twenty minutes. When they were over, the parents all spoke about how wonderful it was to talk to their children about things they felt passionately about.

Virginia also noticed that students solidified their knowledge when they spoke to their parents. Ali, for example, had selected a review from *The National Post* and one from a magazine that was given away in theatres so patrons could have something to read while waiting for the movie to begin. He found that reviewers in both these publications used a similar formula for writing about movies but that the free magazine never said anything negative about a film. It was, he thought, the function of the free magazine to act as an advertisement for upcoming movies in that theatre and as such was biased. Thus, he was using one piece of knowledge to create meaning for a specific experience. He told his parents that he had acquired this insight for himself and was presenting it to them as a gift.

Parents were quick to respond positively; they expressed gratitude to be involved at such a level. And because of the success of the conferences, parents started to become allies at home. They helped their children find examples of and discussed with them the various types of writing their children were collecting or creating. Thus, they became participants in their children's learning, and they felt empowered by the experience. The principal told Virginia that the office was receiving positive responses about this approach. Students' classroom behaviour was better this year than it had ever been. The students felt that they were a real part of the assessment process. They also felt that Virginia knew them better than the other teachers did. And Virginia benefitted by getting to know her students' parents.

Student-Teacher Conferencing

Virginia was dreading the end of term. Everything up to now had been going great! Students were working on their portfolios, excited about their collections, and full of new knowledge. She knew this through observation, questioning, class discussions, and regular glimpses into her students' portfolios. But now she was expected to assign each student a mark. How should this mark be determined?

The success of the parent-student conference had left her with a germ of an idea. Why not have the students present their work to her in the same way they presented it to their parents, only now it would no longer be a work in progress but a completed piece? The students could use any method they wished to present the work, as long as it could be done within half an hour. Most of the course objectives had already been met, and Virginia had used a checklist to calculate the formative grade for each student. The grades were high, as the students had met almost every objective to the expected standard. But now it was time for the summative assessment: the calculation of the final mark.

Virginia set to work designing a rubric to help her grade the students' work. This rubric was constructed as a table with rows representing the elements of learning and columns representing a level of achievement. The columns followed the ICE model: *I* was Ideas; *C* was Connection; and *E* was Extension. If the students could demonstrate that they had the ideas regarding the construction of a movie review, for example, but that was all they could demonstrate, they were given a passing grade for the movie-review objective. If students provided an example of a movie review or had written one that connected their review to each of the parts of a standard movie review, they were assigned a better grade. If they could extend their knowledge about movie reviews to help make meaning for themselves, personally, as Ali had done, they would be placed at an even higher level for movie reviews. The parent conferences and constant in-class monitoring by peers and by the teacher made it almost impossible for students to work at less than a passing level.

Soon after the middle of the term, once Virginia had finished designing her new method, she gave the students a copy of the rubric. (She would be able to give out the rubric at the beginning of the term next time.) Each student's portfolio requirements had an ICE assigned, so that the students knew prior to the conference what was required and, more importantly, what level they were at. While many students were content with the level they had earned, those students who wished to raise their level knew precisely how to do it. All that was left was the conference itself, the moment the portfolio was presented.

For Virginia, it was the best June she had ever had in teaching. While her colleagues complained about marking, Virginia was feeling free to enjoy her students, who treated the conference experience as a conversation between two equals. Virginia learned a lot, laughed a lot, and more than once was moved to tears. Her students had selected examples of writing styles that had personal meaning. Many had made extensions and were achieving a superlative grade; these extensions were "natural, personal" extensions that Virginia, their parents, and their peers had helped them make.

The students were aware that the assessments would be transferred into marks for their report cards. The grades ranged between a 95 (superlative) and a 50 (a passing grade), and just a passing grade was rarely given. Virginia built a Wow! factor into the conference, which was reserved for any student who wanted a 100. Not only would the student have had to achieve a superlative rating on every piece, but also the presentation had to have a feature in it that made Virginia say Wow! Several students used the conference to become exceptionally creative. One student, Alain, created a five-minute video called "From the Back Row," in which he reviewed a movie recently released on DVD and in which he used actual film clips. Virginia said Wow! and Alain achieved a 100.

CONCLUSIONS

Virginia likes the marking she does now. More importantly, she likes the way her students have responded to her new method of assessing. Her students are happy, active, and motivated to move forward to the next steps in their learning. They feel that they have real choice in how they are assessed. Their portfolios provide them with options and ideas for next steps. The ICE model provides a fair structure: students who have the information will pass; students who move forward with the information will excel.

Not only are students and teachers happy. Parents, too, are happy. The conferencing experience gives them a glimpse into what their children are doing in school and informs them about their children's progress. And the administration is happy. They are getting positive feedback from students and parents. Everyone is happy, in fact, and this is so primarily because the method of assessment that Virginia worked out demonstrates that students met all the expectations that were set for them. And very little marking was required to show it.

Learning about Assessment with Primary Children

2

TIMOTHY MOSSER

SCENARIO

Jacob was eager to embark on his first permanent teaching position. With his long-range plans developed, the learning materials prepared, and his classroom brightly decorated, Jacob welcomed his Grade 1 class to school on the first day. During lunch, five-year-old Maddie proudly announced to the class that she knew how to count to 110. Her peers were very impressed, which instantly sparked a series of discussions about how high everyone could count until Jacob overheard Paul quietly remark, "I never knew numbers went so high."

At that moment, Jacob realized that one of his first tasks would involve assessing the wide range of academic strengths and skills that each of his twenty-four students brought into his classroom. As well, with the first round of report cards and parent-teacher conferences scheduled to begin after Thanksgiving, he felt that he needed to clearly develop strategies for assessing not only early strengths but also growth in a way that would be easy for parents to understand and administrators to accept. How could this be done, and by October?

WHAT YOU WILL LEARN IN THIS ESSAY

- that there is a wide variety of "assessable moments" in any classroom environment;
- that methods and practices for clear assessments are transferable to junior, intermediate, or senior learning environments;
- that including primary students in the overall design (e.g., self-assessments, peer-assessments) helps improve a teacher's own understanding;
- how critiquing and questioning assessment methods used by others is helpful.

DISCUSSION

Jacob had always been surrounded by children, whether working as a summer camp counsellor in the local sports camp or tutoring math twice a week at home. His decision to pursue a teaching career was a natural next step after graduation.

Receiving a contract in late summer from his local school board was a dream come true. While he had been prepared to gain in-class experience by supply teaching, the opportunity to have his own Grade 1 class was a pleasant surprise. With September just around the corner, Jacob immediately made arrangements to meet with his new principal.

His new principal, Liz Miles, had been working in education for twenty-two years. She had moved into the field of administration early in her career, when new schools were emerging faster than school boards could staff them. As a classroom teacher and administrator, Liz had witnessed many changes and trends in how children are taught, how teachers are prepared, and the values that are promoted each year as political climates change.

The prospect of joining Liz's staff team intimidated Jacob more than slightly. Mrs. Lansing, the former Grade 1 teacher, was a bit of an icon and was much loved by all who knew her. At their meeting, Liz explained, "We are a small school with very well-established families. Many of the new Grade 1 students have siblings who had Mrs. Lansing when they were in Grade 1. Mrs. Lansing was wonderful! We were all very sad to say goodbye when she retired. I know that all of the parents were very comfortable with her methods and her overall approach to learning."

Walking back to his empty classroom, Jacob realized now, more than ever, that he had much to prepare. Not only was he about to officially launch his teaching career, but, on top of that, he had fewer than twelve days to set up his classroom, prepare his learning materials, and submit his long-range plans. He had not anticipated the additional burden of filling the shoes of a seasoned veteran who was deeply admired by students, parents, and staff. The next few weeks were going to be busy!

When he finished preparing, Jacob stood in the middle of a swirl of colour and light, and he quietly admitted that he had surprised himself. Creating an inviting space for his Grade 1 students under such a time constraint hadn't been an easy task, but somehow he had managed. Seats were arranged in small groups; evocative bulletin boards with simple text were displayed; even the class calendar happily announced that it was September to any visitor. Jacob felt ready.

At the end of the first week, Jacob received a brief note from Liz: "Thanks for the long-range plans. Hope your first week went well. Please forward your assessment plans when you have a chance." Jacob was confused. Included in his long-range plans were specific goals and outcomes for each unit. It seemed obvious to him that his students would achieve the required skills just by participating in the daily program. In a later discussion, Liz clarified her request: "Any curriculum plan needs to include a plan for assessment. It's not enough to simply organize your units throughout the year and expect your students to progress. "A plan for assessment," repeated Jacob as he walked away. Despite all his preparations, Jacob suddenly felt very far behind.

Throughout his practice-teaching rounds, Jacob had many chances to observe different primary programs in action, and he had the luxury of adopting those elements that he particularly liked. So, from opening exercises to tidy-up routines, Jacob established his own program. Following his discussion with Liz, he found himself revisiting his observations during practice teaching and recalled the advice that he received from a thirty-year veteran in the primary division. In Jacob's opinion, Ray Wilcox had seen it all. When Jacob asked Ray about how he assessed and graded his students, Ray offered his honest and direct opinion:

> When it comes time to plan assessment, formal tests and grades can't be your only concern, especially with Grade Ones! We have to consider all means by which we gather information about how kids learn and what they have learned. It will always be easier to hand out a test. Just as there will always be people who teach to the test, the difference between teaching and testing appears when you dig deep to find the time and energy to observe, ask questions, document, and create dialogue between students, teachers, and parents. There are no limits to assessable moments! It's not the easy way out, but no one ever said that teaching is easy!

Jacob wasn't surprised by Ray's advice. As a professional with years of experience, Ray prided himself in perfecting his practice, and it showed every day. Jacob, however, was more concerned with how he would balance the demands of teaching the curriculum, satisfy parents and administration, and at the same time maintain a positive and engaging environment where kids want to learn. In fact, one of Jacob's biggest fears was compromising the Grade 1 experience: What if my commitment to evaluate forces out subject matter that isn't formally tested? What will happen to music, art, and drama? What if I lose the freedom to make the best curriculum choices about content and method for my students? While Ray reminded Jacob of the importance of maintaining a balance in his classroom among different methods of assessment, Jacob knew, in his heart, that standardized tests are a reality: How can I familiarize my students with the concept of formal assessment without undermining their love of learning? There must be a balance between demonstrating mastery-level understanding and drills. At a time when he was looking for answers, more questions seemed to be popping up.

In an effort to ground himself in the face of a dizzying debate, Jacob recounted the methods of assessment that he was already familiar with: observations, pre- and post-tests, interviews, formal tests, checklists, self-assessments, samples of student work.

Observations

Observation as a method of assessment was very familiar to Jacob. In fact, when he was a pre-service-teacher candidate, it was observation that allowed Jacob to critique the practices of his associate teachers. He jotted down some rough notes, which allowed him to both remain involved with the daily program and remember terrific teaching ideas as they appeared. And in the setting of his own classroom, Jacob found himself designing his program and the space within the classroom to allow for opportunities to observe students throughout each day. For example, he could easily see that small-group activities with student leaders highlight six-year-old Becky's tendency to dominate a discussion. Jacob was in a good position to monitor and make specific notes relating not only to Becky's social habits but also to her preference to use manipulatives when subtracting.

Pre-Tests and Post-Tests

As a means of establishing a baseline for new students, pre-tests allowed Jacob to compile an inventory of students' strengths and identify potential weaknesses early in the school year. As he dealt with the intensity of September (e.g., new students, shifting class sizes, anxious parents), he had to find time to spend with each student and continually monitor the behaviour and activities of others. Jacob was able to take considerable comfort knowing that time spent with pre-testing was time well-spent, as he was then able to make reference to these early-September scores during the first round of parent-teacher interviews. Jacob chose to use pre-test scores to assess a child's ability to recall the name and sound of individual letters and numbers, recognize words on sight, and identify basic mathematical concepts.

Figure 1 shows one student's attempt to complete a pre-test that requires the printing of numbers up to 100 in sequential order. This pre-test is meant for Grade 1 students at the beginning of the school year. This student is unable to print numbers beyond twenty-one, is confused with multiples of ten (prints reversals), and prints some figures backwards.

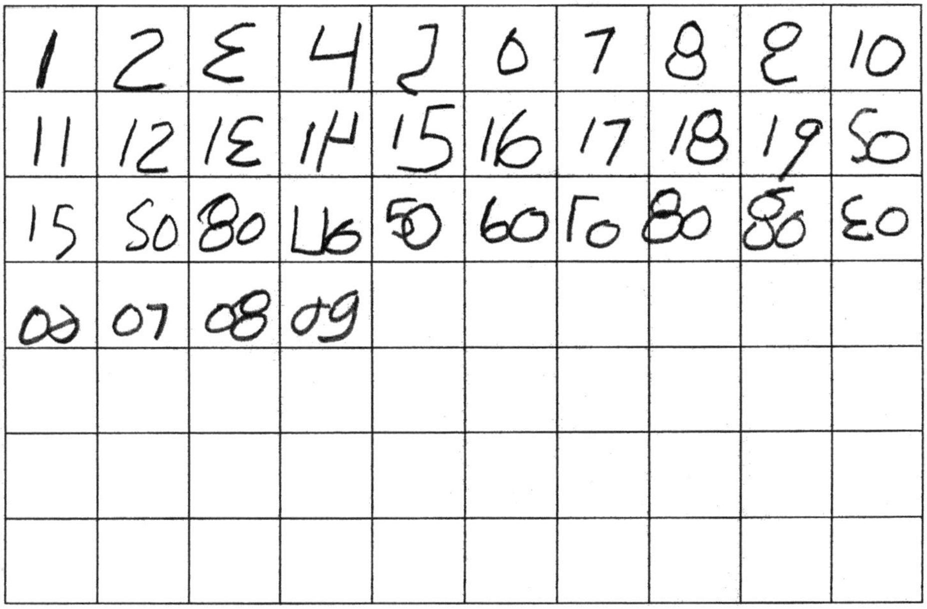

Figure 1. A Grade 1 student's attempt to print numbers up to 100 early in the school year

As the year unfolded, Jacob administered the test several more times (post-tests) and compared the results with the first one. The comparison monitored the improvement of each student. By the next round of parent-teacher conferences, Jacob was able to identify exactly when his students mastered specific skills. Along with in-class assignments and homework, the pre-tests and post-tests provided a meaningful and easy-to-understand portfolio of student growth.

Interviews

One of Jacob's fondest memories from his own experience in school came from his days as a student in Grade 1. While he couldn't recall many specifics, he did remember that each Monday his teacher, Mrs. Williams, would invite him to "visit" at her desk. While she often asked about his weekend, his dog, and the most recent adventures of his little sister, Mrs. Williams would also have a question or two about a piece of work that Jacob had completed the week before. It was many years after their Monday visits that Jacob fully understood their purpose. While she was analyzing, observing, clarifying, and recording—that is, undertaking valuable formative assessments—her students were enjoying their own special time with her. It was this memory of caring and interest that Jacob wanted to pass along to his students.

Unfortunately, finding time to meet individually with each student is a tremendous challenge for most teachers. And Jacob was no different; as he began his career, Jacob found it next to impossible to visit with each student during the day. Frustrated but still hopeful, he decided to place a call to Mrs. Williams. She was instantly supportive and encouraging as she offered the following advice:

> No one can do it all in their first year. You might want to consider one area to focus on and really go after it. Once you are comfortable with your results, choose something else. If you don't make some early choices, you will end up worrying about everything and accomplishing very little. Have you thought about establishing a meeting schedule to span the entire week? There is no reason why you have to meet with all of your students on any single day. Don't forget that the purpose of meeting is to gain insight about how the children are performing and also...why? It wasn't a coincidence that you and I met every Monday. Your last name starts with A! For me, the system operated by the alphabet!

As September unfolded, Jacob slowly discovered natural opportunities to create times for visits. For example, Jamie tended to eat his lunch quickly and always had some time on his hands before lunch recess. Jacob used this opportunity for a few minutes of "visiting" and was always ready to end each session with a question or two about some recent samples of Jamie's work.

The value of taking the time to ask questions was most apparent when he was chatting with Sara. He had noticed that she rarely chose to add colour to her illustrations, and, because of this preference, she appeared to be rushing her work. Their visit instantly explained what Jacob had failed to observe in any other way:

> "Sara, I was wondering if you could tell me more about your pictures."
>
> "What do you mean?"
>
> "Well, sometimes it looks like you are rushing your pictures. Is it important for you to be the first person finished?
>
> "No."
>
> "Do you think that you could take some more time with your colouring by adding more details?"
>
> "Okay. It's just that winter is my favourite season, and there really isn't a lot to colour in my winter pictures."

Formal Tests

Jacob's personal experience with formal testing had been largely negative. Any memory relating to test-taking rekindled feelings of stress, anxiety, and last-minute study sessions. As soon as he decided to pursue teaching as a career, Jacob vowed to find a better way to evaluate than test as he had been tested.

At the same time, Jacob knew that his students would soon be facing the reality of a standardized testing program. Furthermore, he had already heard that the administration was considering a split Grade 2-3 class for the next year. His students were going to experience "testing" whether or not he prepared them for it.

The first thing that Jacob decided to do was change the name. He no longer mentioned the term "test" in his classroom. Instead, his class had weekly "check-ups."

> "Mr. Abrams, do we have tests in Grade 1? My brother is in Grade 5 and he has tests all the time. He says they are really hard."
>
> "Some teachers call them tests, but I call them check-ups. Just like when you visit your doctor to see how your body is doing, in Grade 1 we have check-ups to see how your brain is doing! Most of the time they aren't hard unless you haven't been practising."

And so it began. Each Wednesday, Jacob's class had their weekly check-up, based on material that they were covering. Some weeks the class did spelling, while other weeks they were asked to recognize different coins by identifying their value. It was a huge hit! By the end of the first two weeks, the class had even developed their own set of stretching exercises prior to their check-up. Not only had Jacob redirected any apprehension toward testing, but he had also established a weekly routine that would nicely supplement the students' portfolios and closely monitor their growth throughout the year.

Checklists

The concept of teaching with a checklist had always made Jacob shudder. He knew how many hours he had devoted to his long-range and daily plans (which did not include checklists), and any suggestion that might result in straying from his plans did not sit well with him. Jacob did not know that by organizing the skills to be taught during the year in the form of a checklist would streamline his plans; he had always thought checklists would compromise the integrity of his program and be tantamount to "teaching to the list." He did not know that checklists could enhance not only his teaching but also his students' learning.

Checklists are a great boon to teachers in assessing complex skills; they itemize individual elements of a larger, more complex expectation. A teacher's checklist of curriculum-based skills and student performance is what supports the assessment rubric, a very important instrument for making their criteria known and understood by students and parents before specific work begins. (For the purposes of this essay, a rubric is defined as an elaborated description of what each level of the performance means in terms of characteristics. Often rubrics also specify the categories in which these descriptions are appropriate.)

Working within a rubric like the one defined above, students learn to recognize the various achievement levels within specific tasks. Opportunities to take control of their own learning often seem to appear spontaneously, as students learn the difference between just satisfying teacher expectations and exceeding them. At the same time, students learn to accurately identify their own needs for improvement. When Jacob began including rubrics in his assessment plans, he gained confidence in his ability not only to satisfy the expectations of his principal and better inform his students' parents but also to provide his students with their earliest experience in becoming their own evaluators.

Self-Assessments

By the end of their first term together, Jacob and his students established a firm rapport. At the same time, their strength as readers was blooming, and Jacob felt that the introduction of models for self-assessment at this point would only help readers bloom even more. Furthermore, his students would already be familiar with the concept of following printed instructions to guide them through their learning.

Introducing self-assessments would also provide considerable feedback to Jacob as he learned more about his students' most and least favourite elements of the unit. He would also be in a good position to critique his own teaching style as students shared their thoughts. For example, one student said, "I really liked acting out our play, but all of the practising was boring. My group was ready after the first day!"

As students complete their self-assessments, both in class and at home, Jacob can monitor student growth and thereby create dialogue among parents, teachers, and students. During the first-term parent-teacher interviews, Jacob found that by including samples of his students' self-assessments in their portfolios, the dialogue naturally flowed to include both highlights and concerns.

> Vicki's Mom: "It's really interesting that Vicki indicated that she didn't enjoy illustrating her most recent research project when that was one area where both her dad and I praised her for going above and beyond what was required in September."
>
> Jacob: "I'm glad that you noticed that change because I was hoping to spend some time tonight to discuss her attitude as I have observed it in the classroom over the past few weeks."

Samples of Student Work

Throughout his teacher training, Jacob had become familiar with the concept of gathering samples of his own work and combining them to form a portfolio. In fact, developing a portfolio to show growth was deemed so important by the Faculty of Education that it became an embedded expectation in the form of a course credit. Jacob continued to add to his professional portfolio well after graduation, and he was excited about having his students build portfolios of their own.

In his opinion, portfolios were the best format in which students and teachers alike could present their own best thinking and their most creative work, not the thinking and work prescribed by others. A cumulative record of student growth in the form of portfolios seemed like a logical approach in a primary classroom where test scores (excluding pre-test inventories) were simply not a reality. And Jacob thought it important that a wide range of materials be included in each portfolio; for example, digital photos of science experiments in action, video footage of gym class, and tape recordings of early reading experiences were all wonderful ways to supplement a standard collection, which were usually printed materials and notebooks.

CONCLUSIONS

As the year unfolded before him, Jacob simply couldn't wait to move ahead! Now, with a wide range of models to choose from, Jacob was feeling well prepared to design an assessment model that met the academic and social needs of his students, the expectations of his principal—and all within a comfortable structure that parents could understand. The puzzle pieces were coming together. After reflecting on the range of advice and opinions that he received from veteran colleagues and his own observations, Jacob realized now more than ever that teaching is a highly personalized profession.

Accommodating and Assessing Students with Exceptionalities 3

LYN SHULHA AND CHRISTOPHER DELUCA

SCENARIO

Cara and Gavin are new teachers at Governor Simcoe High School in Ontario. Cara has been assigned various levels of Grade 9 and 10 science, and Gavin has similar assignments in math. One Monday in late September, Gavin and Cara both get a note in their mailboxes requesting that they be present at a meeting to discuss a recently completed individual educational plan (IEP) for one of their students, Josh. The school is required to have in place such a plan for any student diagnosed with a learning difficulty, and teachers are expected to modify their instruction and assessment practice based on the plan.

WHAT YOU WILL LEARN IN THIS ESSAY

- what complexities are inherent in delivering special education;
- what resources are available for teachers to help with assessment;
- what accommodations are possible within typical schools;
- what policies and practice related to special education can accommodate exceptional learners.

DISCUSSION

Cara and Gavin are beginning teachers. Until now, their contact with each other at school had been limited to conversations about school policies and routines. Their only other school-based interactions have been social. They did talk to each other for a while at the opening staff barbecue, and they both have signed up for the teacher super-all-star team, made up of faculty who can be counted on when school athletic teams are looking for competition.

As Gavin prepares for the meeting, he begins thinking about the seven students in his three classes whom the school has "identified" for him. He already knows that he has exceptional students because he received a folder during his second week of school with copies of their IEPs. He is feeling guilty now that he hasn't done anything with this information. "But," he rationalizes, "this has been a whole month of new tasks, and I wanted to get to know my students without the labels that others may have attached to them."

Josh will be an addition to his group of exceptional students. Gavin had never been to one of these debriefing meetings and was unsure about what to expect, and so it was reassuring to enter the office of the coordinator of special education on the designated day and see Cara already at the table.

All four of Josh's teachers for this semester are given a copy of Josh's plan. As they glance over it, they are informed by the coordinator that Josh's exceptionalities were primarily communicative, meaning that there were no physical, developmental, or emotional contributors to Josh's exceptionality. In fact, the process of identifying Josh and creating this plan had come about primarily because his parents and some of his teachers from last year were convinced that there was a significant discrepancy between Josh's intellectual ability and his achievement. The pressure of their concerns had finally helped in qualifying Josh for an individual placement review.

Gavin glances at Cara, who is reviewing the Statement of Needs section of the form. Josh, his parents, and the special education teacher have singled out the following needs for special attention:

- to increase on-task behaviour;
- to increase confidence and self-esteem in academic abilities;
- to use leadership abilities in constructive ways;
- to develop reading speed and fluency;
- to develop organizational skills in written language;
- to develop coping strategies to suit his learning style.

Josh's profile described him as:

- a spatial learner;
- artistic;
- athletic;
- proficient in computer skills.

Gavin reads the results of a standardized intelligence test that Josh has taken: the Wechsler Intelligence Scale for Children (WISC). His overall score in intelligence falls in the sixty-seventh percentile. The special education coordinator indicates that this score is "very good." Gavin is not sure why a 67 is "very good" but thinks that maybe he'll ask about that later. Josh's performance scores are in the "high average" range but his verbal scores are "low average." Josh's visual-motor channels of learning are significantly stronger than his auditory, vocal ones. Again Gavin wonders what this means in terms of classroom behaviour and performance.

All Josh's courses are listed at the bottom of the IEP page. Beside each is the teacher's name and the note, "Josh will be exposed to the regular grade curriculum. Activities that accommodate for needs and allow for success will be provided when appropriate." The coordinator explains that there is no need for any of Josh's teachers to modify the academic expectations that have been laid out in the formal curriculum.

The remainder of the meeting focusses on the specific accommodations to teaching and assessment that are listed on the form. Teachers are to provide opportunities for hands-on work, cooperative work, and computer work. They are also asked to build assignments in which Josh can experience continuous short-term success. There are also stipulations about assessment. Teachers are asked to avoid rote learning and recall instruments. Recommended strategies included the integration of visual presentations, performance assessment, portfolio assessment, and assignments tied to the Internet, as well as increased time for test-taking, prompts for drawing Josh's attention back to the assessment task, and preferential seating for test-taking.

Later, walking to their cars, Cara confesses to Gavin that, while she understands in theory Josh's problems and the strategies they are being asked to use to accommodate his exceptionality, she has no clue how to integrate all of the information into her regular teaching style. Gavin reveals that he had not even identified Josh as an exceptional student. Up until now he has given only two math tests; Josh had failed one of them, and Gavin had attributed this to the fact that Josh was a bit of a class clown and just had not yet settled down to work.

The next day in the hallway, Gavin asks Cara whether she has made any headway on how to deal with Josh. "Not yet. Do you want to get together and talk about it?" They quickly discover that their schedules make it impossible to meet during lunch or a planning period. "Well, how about after school then," suggests Cara. "Just for twenty minutes or so. I've got lots of prep to do," responds Gavin. They agree to meet in one of the science labs that afternoon. It is a place where they can spread out their curriculum plans and the IEPs for the other students in their courses.

This first meeting lasts almost an hour. The first thing Gavin and Cara do is look at the range of accommodations they are supposed to be providing. They discover that many of the recommendations for the other exceptional students overlap with the ones designed for Josh. For example, two other students require that learning be "chunked," that is, limitations be placed on the number of expectations that have to be attended to at any one time. Several others are to be allowed extra time for reading and writing. Most of the exceptional students were targeted as needing help to develop independent work habits and taking responsibility for their own learning. But, while the IEPs provided some guidance on how to plan for instruction, guidance for assessment was far from specific. All the plans read the same way—namely that progress toward expectations would be done through daily work, tests, reports, and assignments.

Both Cara and Gavin have summative paper-and-pencil tests planned for the units they are currently working on. They decide that their first step is to figure out how to structure these tests to work better for their exceptional students. Every idea they entertain seems to have an accompanying pitfall. For example, if they gave these students more time for test-taking, other students might think it unfair. If they gave these students a different test, it might be impossible to compare how students have achieved the expectations. If they gave their exceptional students an open-book test to avoid focussing on recall, the other students might say it was cheating. Cara and Gavin feel as if they're getting nowhere. They wonder whether accommodation of assessment practices for exceptional students was really a practical idea after all. If they adjusted the way they taught and tested to help the exceptional students, wouldn't they be disadvantaging the others? Shouldn't they be concerned for all the students in their classes? And what is a "communication exceptionality" anyway?

Finally, Cara and Gavin realize that this dilemma is not solvable in a single meeting. They need some new ideas if they are to help their exceptional students without being unfair to the others. They decide that a good starting point would be to revisit the nature of exceptionalities and their responsibilities as teachers. They book another meeting for the end of the week. Cara agrees to look up some of the definitions of exceptionalities and to see what the formal roles and responsibilities of teachers are in responding to these students. Gavin volunteers to look through the resource guide they received from the school district on how to think about assessment.

Their second meeting is spent not only sharing what they have found but also in making sense of the new information in the context of what they already know about Josh and the other students in their classes. Cara found that an exceptional pupil is defined as "a pupil whose behavioural, communicational, intellectual, physical or multiple exceptionalities are such that he or she is considered to need placement in a special education program by a committee" (OME, 2000, A3). Cara shows Gavin the definitions of each of the exceptionalities identified by the Ontario Ministry of Education. She has highlighted a section that repeats the description that the special education coordinator had used when talking about Josh. It is apparent that Josh has what is officially considered a "learning disability" (A19). Cara reports that a learning disability manifests itself as a special case of communication exceptionality. It can be both academic and social and is related to information-processing. It now makes sense to Gavin and Cara why issues of confidence, self-esteem and independence had been clustered with concerns over reading, writing, on-task behaviour, and learning styles.

Cara points out the seven responsibilities listed in the Ontario Ministry of Education document for every teacher who is working with an identified exceptional learner. One causes Cara to react a bit: "Communicates the student's progress to parents" (A9).

She isn't surprised that she will have to report to parents. She knows about the scheduled mid-semester parents' night and her chance to spend ten minutes to report student progress to every parent who shows up. But, in reading this extract, Cara recalls that it was Josh's parents who had been instrumental in trying to help him be more successful at school. Both parents had come to the conference to help develop Josh's plan. Maybe "communicating progress" in this case was intended to mean something different from what she had previously thought. Maybe all the parents of students identified as exceptional had some other expectations of her.

Gavin, too, arrives with highlighter applied throughout his district handbook on assessment. But, before opening it, he pulls out a copy of another government policy document. He had put a double star beside the following sentence: "The primary purpose of assessment and evaluation is to improve student learning" (OME, 2000, 13). Gavin is excited about his discovery. He goes into great detail about how attention to this policy statement could help them begin conversations with their students. He suggests that they discuss with the students at the outset why various forms of assessment could take place within a single unit of work and why some students might be assessed in a different way from the way others are.

Cara listens attentively, but she is not convinced. "You want to negotiate with students the way we do assessment in our courses?" she asks. Gavin suggests that they could at least start thinking about that as a possibility. But Cara has more questions: If we focus our assessments on learning, how will we determine grades? If we don't use our assessments for grades, how will we get the students to do the work? If we do more assessment, when will we have time to teach?

Finally, Cara challenges Gavin to describe how they could be expected to both identify and report on all of the accommodations they are to make for their students and provide grades on how well the formal curriculum expectations have been met. Do we give separate grades? Should we find a way to combine this information?

These are difficult questions, and they are ones that Gavin has no answers for. But he is convinced he has come across an important policy and that down the road it might be useful in helping him and Cara to structure new practices.

Gavin reaches for his assessment handbook. In it he had highlighted sections that demonstrated strategies for helping all students generate goals of learning that could be blended with official curriculum expectations. These goals included gathering information, managing information, taking notes, solving problems, evaluating peers, evaluating oneself, and being better prepared for tests.

At this point, Cara and Gavin notice that it is approaching 5:00 p.m. Not only is it getting late, but, as well, their brains are hurting! They look at their schedules and realize that it would be another week before they could meet again. Gavin says he is interested in pursuing questions about whether a teacher who has exceptional students should be testing for curriculum content or skill development. Cara wants to follow up on parents' expectations of the school and of the teacher. As they mull over where they might find this information, they realize they have overlooked the obvious—Why not have their next meeting with the special education coordinator?

Gavin sets up the meeting, and one day the following week, after school, he and Cara arrive in the special education coordinator's office. They bear their latest resources. They first have some specific questions to ask:

> C: Someone told me that you've been a teacher for twenty-seven years. How long have you been doing special education?
>
> SEC: This is actually my eighth year full-time, but I had four years of part-time experience when I was gathering qualifications that would later let me work in the area full-time. During those years I was on a steep learning curve, what with taking courses and trying to apply what I was learning here at school.
>
> G: Ever since we had that meeting with you about Josh, Cara and I have been trying to figure out what we should actually do in our classrooms. So far we've just ended up with more questions.
>
> C: We're not even sure we need to focus on questions of special education at this point. It's interesting, all right, but we're still working at getting our regular teaching patterns in place. We thought maybe you could give us some strategies that we could just adopt for now.
>
> SEC: Well, I certainly have some ideas and resources that you're welcome to, but I wouldn't want you to go away thinking that there's a set formula for this kind of work. Almost all exceptional students are now part of regular classrooms. This means that you will need to develop a plan for

instruction and assessment that is likely quite different from what you experienced as a high school student. Before mainstreaming became the norm, it was possible for teachers to imagine that they had a homogeneous group of learners in front of them. This was never true, of course. But when I started teaching it was easy to think that my job was to teach the curriculum content—usually in the way that made the most sense to me—and then, at reporting time, to sort my students into categories, ranging from those who had learned the most to those who had learned the least. I would base my decisions and rankings on test scores that, at the time, I believed were objective.

Looking back, I realize that I thought my tests were good because they made sense to me. What working in special education helped me see was that often my top students were at the top because the way they learned was compatible with the way I taught. In other words, my best students were most like me! Today, 10 to 20 percent of some of our classes have students identified as exceptional. In some schools it is even higher. This makes setting out a single path to achieving the curriculum a problem. We have to recognize that such a path is going to frustrate both those who are capable of forging ahead creatively and on their own and those who tend to act out or fall behind because they find it difficult to grasp their teachers' approaches to instruction and assessment.

G: Do you see classroom practice changing?

SEC: I see many teachers working hard at modifying their instruction. They work at clarifying the instructions and expectations they have for any given task, reducing the amount of information they expect exceptional learners to carry around with them, creating checklists so that progress towards expectations is evident, and being flexible in the order and time frame in which students are required to meet the expectations for each unit. This modification is an important step.

The biggest hurdle from my perspective seems to be assessment. In our school, written tests and assignments are still the predominant way that teachers determine how much students are learning and what their grades will be. Teachers who integrate oral presentations, storyboards, photo journals, portfolios, and computer-generated models into their general evaluation plans are still in the minority, particularly in the disciplines that you teach!

The three of them spend another hour talking about the kind of instructional environment that might lead to the use of these less conventional forms of assessment. Cara wonders if she could ever feel comfortable in giving students some choice in how they might demonstrate their learning. As the conversation continues, Cara and Gavin realize that assessment will look different in Cara's classes than it will in Gavin's: they each have different strengths upon which to build.

Now it is Gavin who begins to feel uncomfortable. Wasn't there a continuing demand from the public to have students' grades be an accurate reflection of how well they have achieved the curriculum expectations? Would parents, even parents of students identified as exceptional, accept these alternate assessment practices and the grades they produced in the same way as they would exam results?

In response, Cara pulls out an article she had found the previous week. The authors had worked for three years talking with special education teachers, administrators, counsellors, students with disabilities, and their parents. The article focussed on the experiences of the parents in fifty-seven families. The researchers had interviewed and surveyed parents about their attitudes toward their children's school programs. The authors talked, in part, about how schools might make the unfortunate assumption that some parents, especially parents in lower-income neighbourhoods, don't interact much with the school. The parents who were surveyed for this article, however, felt strongly that it was important to be involved in designing and in carrying out the programs constructed for their children.

The biggest roadblock for them tended to be the low quality of their communication with the school. The parents who were involved only through the IEP process, teacher conferences, and report cards felt distanced from the process and tended to believe that their suggestions made little difference in the way their children's learning unfolded. On the other hand, the parents who were also connected regularly through phone calls, progress reports, and parent groups learned how to support their children's progress. Cara feels confident about the findings of the article and says, "Maybe one of the keys to using newer approaches to assessment is to get parents regularly involved in their use and in the interpreting of results."

Cara and Gavin leave the coordinator's office with much to think about, more to read, and an invitation to come back any time. Considering that they both have unit tests fast approaching, Cara selects one of the books suggested by the coordinator (Hutchinson), and Gavin takes the other (Friend, Bursuck, and Hutchinson) for some immediate help. They agree that for next week they will each summarize only the sections that could relate to constructing and administering tests. Their plan is to email each other their findings so they can do some practical work the next time they meet. Cara agrees to begin drafting her test using the results of their readings.

Figure 2 shows a draft of the first three questions of Cara's test and indicates her plans for designing it for exceptional students. She learned from the readings that exceptional students often need additional preparation for testing and additional time to complete tests. Bearing this in mind, she created some instructions and two practice questions, each with a different format.

Name ______________________________ Date ____________________

(The date is to help students keep papers organized over the semester—maybe put them in a portfolio?)

Microscope Quiz

(Use fonts that have spaces between the letters.)

(Insert a drawing of a microscope into the space to the left as a reference for those who need to "see" the microscope to talk about its parts and function. Be sure that it is large enough to exhibit the critical parts.)

1. **Match** the parts of the microscope (right) with their use (left). Place a letter in the space provided. You will have one letter left over. **(5 marks)**

(Indicates the contribution of each question to the overall score so students can govern time.)

Regulates the amount of light ______	A. Base
(Allow for space in between items and responses for easier visualizin.)	
Supports the microscope ______	B. Clip
Magnifies the object ______	C. Diaphragm
Brings the object into focus ______	D. Fine adjustment knob
Holds the slide in place ______	E. Objective lens
	F. Stage
	(Place choices in alphabetical order.)

2. **Place an X** beside your answer **(1 mark)**

The total magnification for a microscope with an eyepiece magnification of 10x and an objective magnification of 5x is:

______10x ______15x ______50x ______105x

(Avoid including a distracter—e.g., 500—that could look similar to the correct answer—50 to someone with visual processing problems.)

3. **Circle the letter** beside the correct answer **(1 mark)**

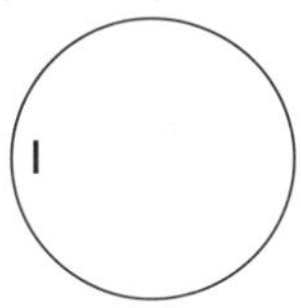

(Include the visual representation of the problem.)

Look at the picture above. The image (I) that you are studying is on the left of your field of vision. Which way would you move the slide to centre the image?

A. Left B. Right

C. Up D. Down

Figure 2. Cara's draft design for testing exceptional students

She plans to go over the instructions and questions with her class the day before the test. After the test she plans to meet individually with her exceptional students to find out what worked or did not work for them. The instructions for the end-of-unit test go like this:

> Tomorrow, I will be passing out two pieces of paper. One is the test. The second is a science crossword puzzle. The test will have eight questions and there will be twenty possible marks. I will set aside thirty minutes for the test. You will be asked to match, select the correct response, label a diagram, and construct two short answers. Some of you will be done much faster than others. If you finish early, you can turn your paper over and move on to the crossword puzzle. You will need your textbook as a resource when you are doing the puzzle, since the words come from our next unit of work. For those of you who would rather catch up on some reading in other courses, you may bring one book to work with until time is up. We will do the crossword puzzles together once the test is over. Now, let's try a selection question and a short-answer question for practice.

Gavin praises Cara's approach. He particularly likes the way she has organized the testing time so that it doesn't appear that the exceptional students are being given more time than the others. When Gavin asks to see her test, Cara produces her plan (see Figure 2). She is eager to show him how her reading has influenced the test format and to see if he has any other suggestions.

Cara gives Gavin her test complete with pencilled-in notes. She tells Gavin that she plans to start a file of these "work-ups" of her tests. She sees now that this might be a way to begin a conversation with a parent who wants to understand how the accommodation process is working.

CONCLUSIONS

Gavin and Cara continued to meet regularly during their first year of teaching. They took advantage of the books provided by the special education coordinator. They found themselves checking through recent educational journals to see if their thinking around adaptations to instruction and assessments was supported by the research community. They found that journals such as *Exceptional Children, Journal of Learning Disabilities, Learning Disability Quarterly, Journal of Special Education Technology,* and *Teacher Education and Special Education* gave them both support for their efforts and good ideas about what to try next.

By December they had established a regular routine for advancing their learning. Every second meeting (about once a month) they met after school at a favourite café. This allowed them to work hard and at the same time enjoy themselves. Their January meeting was celebratory because they had both been successful in recruiting support from their department heads to try out some performance assessments in second semester. Cara experimented with portfolios in a couple of her Grade 10 science units. While she had read a great deal about portfolios, she felt that she needed to test out the idea on a small scale before instituting it more broadly. She hoped that portfolios might ultimately be a useful tool in bringing parents of her students who had been identified as exceptional (and maybe all her parents!) into decision-making about their students' learning and assessment. But that would be for another year!

Gavin was instituting electronic journals in his math classes. Students were using regular journal entries to describe what they were learning about math and to ask questions. Because these journals were constructed on the computer, students had access to pictures, diagrams, drawing tools, and text to help them communicate their new understandings. One feature that Gavin was particularly excited about was the automatic reminder attached to the journal. Two days before an entry was due, each student got an email with the organizing questions for that entry. The next day, a list of students who had not opened their emails would be sent to Gavin, allowing him to follow up with those students. He hoped that this feature would encourage routine building for his exceptional students.

Gavin was looking forward to using these electronic journals both as a formative tool to scaffold the learning of those who required it and as a challenging tool for those who showed deeper understandings in each of the units. When students demonstrated proficiency in the unit's concepts, he recruited them to become part of his on-line response team rather than requiring them to create more journal entries.

Cara and Gavin have made great strides in their thinking about assessment for Josh and for all of their students. Their willingness to work on the school's assessment team next year will no doubt provide them with even more opportunities.

Note: For more about Cara and Gavin's experience with Josh, see Chapter 14.

Using the ICE Model with Learners of Differing Abilities 4

ROBERT PETRICK

SCENARIO

Sana, teaching a Grade 5-6 split class this year, is disenchanted with the prevailing criterion-referenced approach to assessment. While she sees its value for many of her students, it does not work well for those children who are struggling. When she uses only the criterion-referenced approach, she feels that these struggling children, the ones who rarely meet any of the accepted standards of performance, walk out of the building every day convinced they can't learn. Sana expresses the dilemma this way: How can a teacher help all students (those who struggle and those who don't) gain a sense of performance excellence that they can embrace, understand, manipulate, and generalize to all their school work?

WHAT YOU WILL LEARN IN THIS ESSAY

- that students can have ownership, control, and accountability when learning;
- that the ICE model works across the curriculum to provide ownership;
- that students can differentiate among various aspects of knowledge, including "knowing about knowing";
- that there are various elements of a classroom culture that support achievement;
- that there are ways of differentiating achievement so that learners of all abilities can be successful.

DISCUSSION

Using Assessment Positively

Experienced classroom teachers know that each September they can expect to welcome students who vary in many ways. There will be a few budding

Einsteins, some who aren't the slightest bit interested in learning anything useful, some who want to learn but who have one or more impediments, and the rest, who show all sorts of individuality.

All teachers are concerned about making life in the classroom as helpful for one learner as for another. The current reality is, however, that standardized, large-scale tests are used to provide an objective measurement for some parts of students' performances (and, you suspect, yours as well). While there is some value in knowing how your class does compared to others, there is a cost for those who always do poorly on standardized tests.

To help offset these periodic blows to self-esteem that some students experience, teachers can foster a self-sustaining ethic of curiosity, motivation, and empowerment to learn independently on an hour-to hour basis in the classroom. To achieve these things, students need a sense of ownership of their own learning, and this sense is best achieved through an adaptation of the ICE model.

Ownership Control and Accountability

One of the most important parts of a teacher's job is to create a positive classroom culture, that is, provide an atmosphere in which people come together to believe in certain principles: excellence, for example. Teachers need to impart to their students a real sense of control, opportunities to self-evaluate and to exercise the ups and downs of ownership, which in turn enable students to practise mutually supportive relationships with their teachers and, at the same time, make important decisions for themselves. In a positive culture such as this, students will learn for the sake of learning and will identify and pursue excellence generally and consistently for its own sake.

Here is what Sana did to create a positive culture:

> I decided that if I wanted my students to accept seriously a personalized, customized perspective on assessment, I would have to teach them a lexicon of assessment terminology through which they would approach learning with a sense of accountability. In my class, I have adopted and adapted Wilson's developmental ICE model of assessment as the instrument to combine teaching, learning, and assessing. Students come to appreciate the times when they have "ICEed" a piece of work that they are especially proud of.

Other references to the ICE model are presented in this volume, but Figure 3 in this essay describes how Sana's students understand it.

Letter	Stands For	Description
I	Idea	Identifies the basic point of the task. Student should do it accurately and correctly, with no mistakes.
C	Connection	Demonstrates how the student can apply the task to his or her life or the aspect of the curriculum that is being studied (such as a math task linking to a spelling list). To allow for variable interests of the students, keep this option as open as possible. There's no point in learning something if the student can't or won't apply it to other aspects of life.
E	Extension	Polishes the Idea, either visually or conceptually. An extension needs to result in a finished product, created as flawlessly as the student is capable of doing. The important requirement is that the extension relate directly to the original Idea.

Figure 3. Elementary students' understanding of ICE

ICE Leads to Knowing about Knowing

The achievement of an ICE has become a highly sought-after goal in Sana's class, and it has become a challenge for her to keep an ICE available to all students. An ICE can be prescribed by the teacher or conceived of by the student, relatively independently of the teacher. When Sana prescribes an ICE rubric, it may appear as steps on a staircase, the I (as the foundation) on the bottom left:

E Create a daily timetable that includes Harry Potter's new curriculum. Or … (your idea)

C Show how Harry Potter's new curriculum compares with our present curriculum.

I Harry Potter has come to our school to redesign our present curriculum so that it matches a proper wizard school. He needs our suggestions. Suggest some new subjects to study.

A gratifying moment will be the "unanticipated" ICE. The student has had a flash of brilliance, has told you that a possible ICE is forthcoming (subject to negotiation), and could he or she have a little more time to do this? If you have created your assignments so that they are "ICEable," you can expect many of these wonderful scenarios. An ICEable assignment is one in which the students can approach in a basic way and succeed (an I or a C) and that other students can approach in an altogether different and more expansive way (an E). Many assignments in school limit the application of knowledge (the spelling list or the maths sheet), resulting in a formalism that hampers the creation of a culture of meaningful learning.

Part of knowing about knowing occurs during the negotiations with students over the status of an effort. Is the effort an ICE or not? These discussions are conducted in good spirit, but what is actually being spoken about is the quality of what has been learned. We are talking about, debating actually, the issue of knowing about knowing. Nothing is more important and self-sustaining in a classroom culture than having students make sincere commitments to extending their knowledge.

ICE and its Variations

It takes the whole year for students to understand how an ICE works. The teacher can compromise at the beginning of the year by allowing a simple piece of student work to assume the status of an ICE; the same product, later in the year, would not so qualify.

Products can differ both in appearance and in cognitive character. It is part of my emphasis on metacognition that we, teachers and students together, describe and give names to different kinds of ICEs. Look at Figure 4 and note that none of the variations are described in the literature. My students and I invented them, and you can invent yours, too.

CONCLUSIONS

In modifying the standard ICE model, Sana is unique in her approach. Here is what she concluded about her own version of the ICE model:

- There should be no mistakes in the product. With the promise that an ICE is forthcoming, children will take the product back, repair it, and resubmit it. Mistake-free work is essential to receiving an ICE.
- There should be no repeating an ICE. Once a student has attained an ICE, make it clear that he or she is welcome to try the same idea at a later date, but no ICE will be given, except in the case where an original concept is extended.
- There should be no concrete rewards. The achievement of an ICE should remain unsullied by candies or stickers. If concrete reinforcement is a part of your elementary classroom practice, be sure to keep it distinct from ICEs.
- The possibility of an ICE must be accessible to all. Because you have a wide range of abilities in the class, some give-and-take will be necessary. Flexibility is enhanced if the curriculum, and therefore many of the projects, is individualized. Students can easily be made to understand that an ICE is based on growth and not attainment (outcomes-based) or comparison (norm-based). What you accept in

Type of ICE	Definition	Instruction for Creating a Product
The standard ICE	Creation of a product whose extension relates to the original Idea.	Create an algorithm (e.g., 4 x 3.5/2), write a problem as a story, write a problem as a poem.
The textbook ICE	Creation of an ICE that is a spin-off of something taught recently in class.	As a health activity, write a play about bullying, but relate it to the history curriculum.
The multiple ICE	Creation of various ICEes that are not related to each other directly but all of which tie into the original idea or task.	Complete a large assignment, such as a book report, a group project, or a group presentation.
The mega ICE	Creation of an ICE that is larger in effort and scale than basic ICE.	Complete a large end-of-term or end-of-strand project, focussing on polish and innovation.
The double ICE	Creation of an ICE upon another ICE. The second ICE must act as an extension to the original ICE, which now serves as the Idea in the original ICE.	Create a crossword puzzle on computer, using aboriginal vocabulary, then supply an answer key in French. (You put one ICE on top of another.)
The triple ICE	Creation of an ICE on top of a double ICE (satisfies those who can't sleep because they wonder how big the universe really is).	Compose and sing a song, using English and French and focussing on the vocabulary used in the original aboriginal vocabulary puzzle.
The mini ICE (ice cube or potential ICE)	Creation of a small ICE that could turn into a really big one (not really qualifying as an ICE but worthy of recognition).	Make a word search of your spelling list. Illustrate a written answer on a reading assignment.

Figure 4. Variations on the ICE model

October may not be acceptable in April. As students become more comfortable with the ICE model, they easily and willingly raise their expectations by themselves.

- Find ways to relate the ICE approach to parents. They are the ones who will read the report card and try to reconcile, for example, the fact that their child is accomplishing many extensions to his or her work but may still be described as a *C* student. You can help alleviate this potential confusion by incorporating student-led conferences and frequent parent-teacher communications into the reporting process.
- Walk the walk and talk the talk. Remember, it is a positive culture that you are aiming to establish in your classroom. Devise strategies to keep ICEs front and centre. Make posters with slogans. Post rules and show different kinds of ICEs. Formally recognize each and every accomplishment of each and every student. For example, the day can

begin with a "tip of the hat," when all ICEes from the previous day are recognized and explained to the class. For every ICE given, write a short note to the child on the piece of work. These notes become valuable to the student and will support his or her own credibility when student-led conferences are held.

Assessing Both Quality and Quantity of Learning

5

CINDE LOCK

SCENARIO

Dale Massey has always taught Grade 9 mathematics by focussing on the procedures and concepts embedded in the various units of the curriculum. In past years, Dale has taught each unit separately, quizzed the students part-way through, and then tested them at the end of the unit to assess the extent to which they have learned the concepts covered in the course. Students who do well in his course are those who are able to consistently and accurately use all of the procedures and algorithms taught.

This year, Dale wants to introduce some project-based and investigation-style assignments that encourage students to think about and explore the math concepts in more meaningful ways. He wants his students to understand how to apply the math concepts in different contexts and understand how math relates to situations they encounter in their everyday lives. He also wants them to see that mathematics can be "messy": one math problem can be answered well in various ways and with various solutions. While he has a clear sense of the direction he wants to go in his teaching, he is struggling to find a way to assess student work without focussing only on the correctness of students' mathematical solutions.

WHAT YOU WILL LEARN IN THIS ESSAY

- the importance of including both qualitative and quantitative tools to assess student achievement;
- the value of assessing increasing levels of cognitive complexity in student work;
- how "expert" is different from "novice" in both amount of knowledge and complexity of understanding.

DISCUSSION

Dale decides to assign an investigation task to his students and assess after the assignments are handed in. He makes a point of not providing students

	Level 1 50% to 59%	Level 2 60% to 69%	Level 3 70% to 79%	Level 4 80% to 100%
Knowledge and Understanding (understanding of concepts; performing algorithms)	The student: • demonstrates limited understanding of concepts • performs only simple algorithms accurately by hand and using technology	The student: • demonstrates some understanding of concepts • performs algorithms with inconsistent accuracy by hand, mentally, and using technology	The student: • demonstrates considerable understanding of concepts • performs algorithms accurately by hand, mentally, and using technology	The student: • demonstrates thorough understanding of concepts • selects the most efficient algorithm and performs it accurately by hand, mentally, and using technology
Thinking/Inquiry/ Problem-Solving (reasoning applying the steps of an inquiry/problem-solving process)	The student: • follows simple mathematical arguments • applies the steps of an inquiry/ problem-solving process with limited effectiveness	The student: • follows arguments of moderate complexity and makes simple arguments • applies the steps of an inquiry/ problem-solving process with moderate effectiveness	The student: • follows arguments of considerable complexity, judges the validity of arguments, and makes arguments of some complexity • applies the steps of an inquiry/ problem-solving process with considerable effectiveness	The student: • follows complex arguments, judges the validity of arguments, and makes complex arguments • applies the steps of an inquiry/ problem-solving process with a high degree of effectiveness and poses extending questions

Figure 5. Achievement chart for Grades 9 and 10 mathematics (from OME, 2004, 52-55)

with an assessment rubric for their work when he assigns the investigation task. He asks his colleagues in the math department for examples of investigation tasks that they have used in their classes. From the examples provided, he selects a task that requires the students to use a laboratory-style approach (including the development of a hypothesis, the analysis of results, and the discussion of findings) to explore a particular mathematical concept. Dale likes this one because it requires the use of advanced technology and allows performance across the various curriculum strands in the course.

Dale is comforted by the knowledge that Marcia, the colleague who developed the task he has decided to try, will be available to help him as he provides guidance when the students are completing the task and, more importantly, to help him assess his students' work once the assignment is complete.

When the students have completed the investigation task, it is clear to Dale that his usual style of assessing students is incompatible with the goal of the assignment. If he determines students' grades by summing the number of correct (or partially correct) answers that the students provide, he will not be assessing the complexity of thought with which the students have approached the problem. Nor will he be evaluating the reasonableness of their conclusions. In addition, who the students are as individuals and what they bring to the task are now becoming important to the way he assesses his students.

In his efforts to align his teaching with his assessment methods, Dale discusses his concerns with Marcia. Together they look at the assessment rubric that was designed for the course by the Ministry of Education (see Figure 5). Dale and Marcia observe that, as students advance from one level to another on this rubric, their understanding of concepts is expected to increase from "limited" to "some" to "considerable" to "thorough." Similarly, there is an expectation of increasing degrees of consistency and accuracy in the performance of algorithms as they progress. Students achieving at Level 1 in the area of problem-solving are able to follow "simple" mathematical arguments, then ones of "moderate" and "considerable" complexity. By Level 4, students are able to follow "complex" arguments and judge their validity.

Just as principal Sheyla Murray (see Chapter 10) found the use of this evaluative terminology limiting in her reflections on the introduction of a standard rubric in her school district, Dale and Marcia feel that more description would be needed if they were to assess students fairly, given the type of assignment Dale has just asked them to complete. Further description might also improve the development of common understandings (for teachers, students, parents, and administrators) related to what it means to advance from one level of achievement to another. Marcia thinks that the Ministry's rubric might be useful to describe the products of learning but

	Level 1	Level 2	Level 3	Level 4
Qualitative Indicators of Achievement	• Student can understand or recall simple details and ideas.	• Student has a developing interpretation.	• Student begins responding personally.	• Student has developed an extension of understanding to unfamiliar or abstract contexts.
		• Student can understand connections or relationships among ideas and concepts.		
	• Student can express ideas singly, in no particular order.	• Student can combine several ideas or concepts to form solutions if the concepts are related to classes, differences, and relationships.	• Student can form relationships and connections among ideas and concepts in the context of the problem.	• Student can go beyond the information provided and possibly beyond his or her own experience to see knowledge in a general way.
	• Student provides solutions to problems if they look like ones solved already.	• Student can see how some ideas relate to other ideas—in time, in logic, or in relationship.	• Student can make connections within a problem.	• Student can demonstrate deduction and induction.
	• Student can utilize one idea or piece of information when making judgements.		• Student makes connections between ideas and his or her own experience	• Student can hold logically possible alternate conclusions.
	• Student is able to separate some important ideas from less important ideas.		• Student can generalize within a given or experienced context.	• Student responds critically and can possibly extrapolate.
			• Student can show a comprehensive and sophisticated solution, and organization indicates a comprehensive understanding of the problem.	• Student can form general concepts and integrate these into a whole.

Figure 6. The results of Dale and Marcia's brainstorming for qualitative indicators of learning

that Dale needs something in addition to help him see where his students are in their learning.

Dale feels that, for the assessment of student work on the investigation assignment, the logic and depth of reasoning that students bring to the task is just as important as the accuracy with which they perform the algorithms and procedures that flow from their reasoning. Dale believes that it is important to assess not only the judgements that students make about the appropriateness of their conclusions and solutions but also their ability to generalize and extrapolate from these conclusions. As well, Dale is required to assess these objectives, as they are integral components of the new curriculum he is implementing this year.

Provided in Figures 6 and 7 are some of the phrases that Dale and Marcia consider that relate to both the qualitative differences they wish to assess and the advancements students make that are more suitably measured in quantity (or by their quantitative differences in terms of accuracy, consistency, and thoroughness of response).

Dale and Marcia realize that they have only just begun their work in developing a rubric that fairly assesses students in relation to both quality and quantity. One feature they have not yet considered is how the indicators they have identified might be represented across different categories of learning (e.g., knowledge/understanding, thinking/inquiry/problem-solving, communication, application). Nor have they considered how indicators of achievement might differ across the various strands of mathematics (e.g., measurement and geometry, number sense and algebra, relationships). Dale and Marcia also feel that they need to develop specific rubrics related to specific student assignments, but at the same time they worry about confusing the students by including too many assessment tools.

As they consider the work that lies ahead, Dale and Marcia discuss other, new, aspects of assessment that now seem to be pertinent. That is, with the assignment of projects and investigation tasks on the increase in curriculum documents, Dale feels that the students need to be at the centre of this teaching, learning, and assessment process rather than on the periphery. Having just glanced at the products he received from the investigation task he assigned, Dale notices that students' prior knowledge, their other areas of interest, and the factors that motivate them have directly influenced the quality of the product they submit. These factors are something Dale decides to think about further when assigning tasks in the future.

Dale also thinks that incorporating different types of qualitative assessment criteria into his assignments might change how students think about their work. He thinks they would benefit from knowing the assessment criteria prior to doing the work of the project. Perhaps his students might

	Level 1	Level 2	Level 3	Level 4
Quantitative Indicators of Achievement	• Student shows limited understanding of the problem's math concepts and principles. • Student can organize information only in very simple ways. • Student infrequently applies math terminology, symbols, conventions, methodology, and procedures correctly. • Student communicates only very simple purposes. • Student applies concepts and procedures to solve simple problems relating to familiar settings.	• Student shows understanding of some of the problem's math concepts and principles. • Solution may contain serious computational errors. • Student identifies some important elements of the problem. • Student provides evidence of a solution process (may be incomplete or unsystematic). • There is some ambiguity or lack of clarity in explanation or description. • Student explanations may be difficult to interpret. • Student applies concepts and procedures to solve problems of some complexity relating to familiar settings.	• Student demonstrates nearly complete understanding of the problem's mathematical concepts and principles. • Student uses nearly correct math terminology and notations. • Student executes algorithms completely; computations are generally correct but may contain minor errors. • Student provides reasonably clear explanations or descriptions. • Student communicates effectively. • Student presents supporting arguments that are logically sound but may contain some minor gaps. • Student applies concepts and procedures to solve complex problems relating to familiar settings.	• Student understands the problem's mathematical concepts and principles. • Student uses appropriate math terminology and notations. • Student executes algorithms completely and correctly. • Student provides clear evidence of a solution process, and the process is complete and systematic. • Student provides an unambiguous explanation or description of solution. • Student applies concepts and procedures to solve complex problems relating to familiar and unfamiliar settings.

Figure 7. The results of Dale and Marcia's brainstorming for quantitative indicators of learning

even provide him with insights about how to develop assessment rubrics for future tasks.

Sheyla Murray and Angela Tripp (see Chapter 10) argue that the use of a rubric consisting predominantly of quantitative indicators of student learning (such as the achievement chart provided by the Ministry), might be more suitable for summative assessments than formative assessments of student learning. Dale and Marcia come to the conclusion that perhaps both forms of assessment would be improved with the inclusion of both qualitative and quantitative indicators of student achievement. They decide to explore this possibility further in their future teaching and assessment practices.

When Marcia thinks about her strong students, she notes that they approach problems in a way that is qualitatively different from the way that those students who are struggling do. Indeed, it is almost as if some students (the strong ones) have developed a deep and integrated understanding of the concepts they are learning. They can see multiple ways to approach a problem and are not confined to a linear mode of reasoning that is determined by learned steps. She concludes that, as students advance from novice to expert in their learning, it is not just that they are able to "do more" in relation to consistency and accuracy, but it is also that they "do differently."

Strong students, like Albert or Nils, for example, constantly remind Marcia that advanced learners approach a problem differently because they have prior knowledge and understandings that anchor their new learnings. Marcia notices that strong students are constantly saying things like, "We did a problem sort of like that last year." Or, "I wonder if what we learned about in science class would work here, too." Or, "When we were at the cottage last summer, I noticed something like that." Or, "Maybe we could do our project on the computer."

Albert and Nils don't seem as procedure-driven or as task-specific as other students. They are always on the lookout for ways to see a relationship between what is being asked now and something they have done before. Marcia feels that, if she could teach other kids to think like this, they might remember more of what they learned. These strong students approach the problem, the context, and the solution all at the same time; beginning learners do not. Marcia feels that the differences between these different approaches need to be honoured; students should be assessed along a continuum of cognitive complexity.

Dale and Marcia look more closely at the Ministry's achievement rubric used for the Grade 9 mathematics course they are teaching. They know that there are some indicators of qualitative differences in learning embedded in the rubric (e.g., there are references to efficiency, posing extending questions, and judging the validity of arguments); however, they conclude that most of the terminology used in the rubric is quantitative in nature (e.g., the repetitive use of words such as "limited," "some," "considerable," and "extensive").

Dale and Marcia decide to collaborate on the development of an assessment rubric of their own: one that could be used both formatively (to help the learning) and summatively (to summarize what has been learned) throughout their Grade 9 mathematics course and, in particular, for the assessment of students on the current investigation task. Dale is familiar with the ICE model of assessment, and he integrates his understanding of it into his brainstorming with Marcia.

As Dale and Marcia talk about their collaborative project in the staff room, they are pleased to note that other teachers are getting involved in their conversations. It would be exciting if the others continued to participate as they pursue their ideas about assessing both quality and quantity in learning.

CONCLUSIONS

Dale and Marcia began to understand that both quantitative and qualitative indicators of learning have a place in a complete assessment framework for their math students. The quantitative indicators are useful for summarizing a particular achievement. The qualitative indicators help most with more involved tasks, such as investigations. The growth model for the qualitative approaches allows for the demonstration of complex thinking and thinking that demonstrates growth.

Helping Parents Further their Children's Learning

6

ROBERT J. WILSON

SCENARIO

As a brand-new teacher, Samantha (Sam for short) is about to have her first parent-teacher conference. "It's only October!" she complains. Already she has a had a call from Alan's mother asking her what she can do at home to help Alan read better. "He has to be told every fifth word it seems," she said on the phone. "It's been like that all through school. Now he's in Grade 5, and it's still a struggle." Sam's problem is that she wants parents to help their children do well in school, especially in reading and maths, but she doesn't want them reinforcing bad habits. They'll be at the school Tuesday night.

WHAT YOU WILL LEARN IN THIS ESSAY

- that parents can help their children learn;
- that different strategies work for different situations;
- that children should be working harder than their parents on the problem;
- that learning proceeds in stages;
- that the first stage in learning is ideas; these are then connected, and, finally, they are extended.

DISCUSSION

Samantha meets Alan's mother first, before the other parents, and his mother is eager to learn to help.

"Alan is an interesting boy," Samantha begins.

"Yes, he is," Alan's mother responds. "But his reading is not up to standard, I know."

"Well," Samantha says, "maybe we can do something about that."

With only twenty minutes or so before the next parent's appointment, Samantha gives the shortest version of "teaching for growth" that she had ever heard. It is a good thing she had learned it so well as part of her teacher education courses and that she had had a chance to use it in her practicum.

Had she been a fly on the wall in Alan's home, this is what she would have observed when Alan and his mother sat down together to "do reading" together: With the television off, Alan is reading aloud from his book about knights. "The rattle of armour and the shouts of the archers meant that a message had arrived in the...c ... coor ... I don't know what the next word is."

How can Alan's mother answer this question? She could do several things. One would be to tell him that he word is "courtyard" so he can get on with the story and not lose the sense of what he's reading. Another would be to try to get him to "sound it out" so that he could figure out other hard words for himself when she is not around. Still another strategy would be to have Alan just skip over the word because it is not very important to the story's meaning, and he just may be able to pick it up the next time around when the word is used again in another sentence.

All of these strategies are valid, and good teachers (and wise parents) use them all at different times. But when to use which one really depends on the context and what we believe learning to be. For many people, teachers and parents alike, the correct response to Alan would be to tell him the word so that he could finish the story. "Getting it done" is considered by some the same as learning. When going further is not necessary for learning, this approach may be sensible. But the word Alan is stuck on provides a real opportunity for him to learn something more. The word "courtyard" contains two little words, one of which Alan probably knows. Perhaps the conversation could go like this:

"Alan, is there part of the word that you know?" (Pause.)

"Yeah, ... 'yard.'"

"Right. Knights used to ride up to castles and stop in something called a court-yard, a place in front, just like the yard in front of our house. Sometimes, when you get to a hard word, you can see if you know a piece of it, and if you do, that may be enough to catch the sense of it. Anyway, go on with the story."

Now, this notion of learning is more than "getting it done." Alan has been given a strategy—he may have to be reminded of it more than once—that he can use to help make him a more independent reader. On other occasions, sounding the word out would help. Along with a sense of what the word might be, sounding it out could provide enough cues to help Alan solve the problem for himself. This approach may work with "courtyard," but it is less likely than the first solution because "cour" is not an easy sound for anyone, let alone a young child, to pronounce correctly without knowing the word in the first place.

What principles of learning are being illustrated here? The first one is: Knowledge that is useful in more than one place at more than one time is more powerful than knowledge of single things. So, to help someone be a productive learner, it is usually more useful to help them make connections between what they already know and what they are learning. So, when Alan's mother describes the "yard" in the story as being like the "yard" in the front of their house, she is helping her son make such a connection. Good teachers do this all the time.

The second one is: Help children do it for themselves rather than do it for them. When you want to help others, it is almost always better to have them do it while *you* watch than to have *them* watch while you do it. The involvement of the learner is not only a powerful motivator—just watch children work on games and puzzles and video machines to see this in action—but it also encourages the making of the connections.

These connections can be extended beyond just the stories being read at the moment. The notion of chivalry that Alan is reading about can be incorporated into ideas about manners, for example. Why do we want to have good manners, anyway? Why are they significant in a family? Helping Alan integrate his learning into all aspects of his life will help make him inquisitive, will help him find out what his passions are. But how do we keep these theories in mind during the spontaneous, unpredictable occasions when it would be useful?

If we think of single ideas as useful sometimes—Ideas is the word you need—and joining them up as Connections when appropriate that would help and finally seeing them in unique ways as Extensions, we have a simple model, called ICE, that sums up the progression of learning from simple to more complex. Alan's mother realizes that simply telling Alan the word "courtyard" (Ideas learning) will miss an opportunity to make a link to a good strategy (Connections learning), so she uses this level to respond. Later, if it comes up, when he reaches across the table in front of his brother to grab the food he wants, she will remind Alan about the chivalry found in his book on knights and the role that manners play in civilized behaviour (Extensions learning).

Perhaps an example from another school subject will help illustrate this concept. (Connection!) Alan is studying fractions and ratios in mathematics. Unfortunately, most of his homework involves filling in sheets of examples with little application, little connection, to other mathematics concepts or to his life. Here is one example from his worksheet: 40/100 = ?/60. His working out of the problem followed the usual rules of cross-multiplication that he has used with several earlier ones: 40 x 60 ÷ by 100 = 24. Therefore, ? = 24.

Mathematics, especially in school, often features this type of ideas learning. Unless connections are made to something else, the slightest change to the usual ways in which the problems appear on the sheets produces blank stares from the students.

Most adults will have forgotten the rule described above because they likely haven't had to use it since leaving school. But, it could be useful. Say you are travelling by car at about 100 kilometres per hour; you pass a sign that says Mytown 40. How long will it take to get home? Well, 40/100 is about 2/5 of an hour, and 1/5 of an hour is 12 minutes, so 2/5 would be 24 minutes.

Why can only a few people figure this out in their heads? Probably because the mathematics we were taught in school had no obvious connection to everyday life. But, such connections are everywhere; we were not taught that there were such connections. We all learned our times tables, but the problem of why the nine times tables up to ten produce a number whose digits themselves add up to nine (e.g.: 9 times 2 is 18, and 1 plus 8 is 9; 6 times 9 is 54, and 5 plus 4 are 9) will stump most people because we were not taught why the times tables work as they do.

CONCLUSIONS

There is no single right method of helping children learn, and it is important to know which approach to use under which conditions. Powerful learning occurs when the ideas necessary to learning are connected to other ideas or to one's own previous learning and extended to other areas of one's life. Parents can help their children learn, not only in school but also out of school, by helping them make connections and extensions.

Objectivity and Subjectivity in Classroom Assessment

7

SUE FOSTATY YOUNG

SCENARIO

Explaining and rationalizing her assessment practices to her students and their parents had never been a problem when Lesley taught a full schedule of science courses. She took great care to keep detailed records of the results of all tests, quizzes, projects, participation, and attendance. Now that her schedule has been changed to include two sections of senior physical education, she has started to wonder about how to provide objective judgements and grades for her students' performances. Was it possible to be objective in a course that involves so much individual activity and ability? This is the dilemma she will wrestle with as she meets her first class.

WHAT YOU WILL LEARN IN THIS ESSAY

- what the distinctions are between objective and subjective assessment and judgements;
- what the effects are of practices such as: grading effort and participation; "buffer" marks; creating test questions and assignments;
- how objectivity and subjectivity relate to assessment practices;
- what the biases embedded in assessment practices are and what can be done to reduce their effects.

DISCUSSION

Definitions of Objectivity and Subjectivity

Lesley isn't alone in her concerns about being subjective in assessing her students' learning. The ideal method would be easy to implement, allow students an opportunity to demonstrate a full range of the complexities of their learning, and, at the same time, be free from bias. But, in almost every discussion about learning assessment, teachers are likely to hear references to "objectivity" and "subjectivity," and it will become clear that the former is regarded as highly desirable and the latter is regarded as the bane of teachers' existence. Many teachers seem to be on a never-ending quest to be objective. Objective, bias-free assessment is to be trusted; subjective assessment is not.

When an assessment process is described as objective, it is generally accepted that it is rational, reliable, predictable, and free from bias: rational—there will be little emotional investment on the part of the test-constructor and the test-grader; reliable—final grades will be indisputably consistent no matter who or how many independent graders review the responses; predictable—the assessment will be entirely representative of the course content and learning outcomes; free from bias—expectations and criteria for success are known in advance.

When the process is subjective, on the other hand, it is likely to be less rational (there is a high degree of personal investment in the process), less reliable (due to greater variability of acceptable responses dependent on teacher-specific values), less predictable (because of the cumulative effect of each factor), and biased (many of the expectations and criteria for success are unknown until after the assessment). In fact, when teachers discuss objectivity and subjectivity in assessment, it becomes clear that their primary concerns are with the reliability of and biases in the processes.

Another issue has to do with the inclusion of non-achievement qualities in assessment and whether that practice is a good thing. Assigning grades for attendance, class-participation, or effort are some of the ways that teachers might convince lower-achieving students to work harder and might reward higher-achieving students for their perseverance. By grading these factors as well as performance, many teachers hope to provide a more representative picture of their students' achievement.

There is an ongoing debate among educators about the appropriateness of awarding grades for activities that are not about performance. Proponents of this practice argue that offering grades for attendance, participation, and effort is one way to help lower-achieving students improve their over-all grades and perhaps bolster their self-esteem. Dissenters might agree with the argument but also point out that teachers are likely to "buffer" the marks of low-achieving students if their attendance, attitude, and effort are good; they might not be as likely to extend the same consideration to their mid- or high-achieving students. The assignment of grades could then become highly personalized and based on different criteria for different students.

Beliefs about Objectivity and Subjectivity

Tests with multiple-choice, fill-in-the-blank, and true/false formats are generally believed to be objective, that is, the they are marked without bias and emotional investment; the results are accurate and won't fluctuate to any great degree. The high degree of reliability that these kinds of tests produce contributes to a high level of confidence in students, parents, and administrators alike. The confidence is due, in large part, to the security of an answer key based on factual material in the textbook: the answer is either *A*, *B*, or *C*; it's either true or it's false; it's right or it's wrong. These kinds of tests are designed to elicit specific, unambiguous responses. Generally, an answer key is provided and the nature of the tests ensures that most, if not all, answers are verifiable in the textbook or students' class notes. Unfortunately, many teachers and students find these types of tests to be unduly restrictive, as they provide little chance for students to demonstrate much more than their grasp of facts and fundamental concepts.

When we want to offer an opportunity for students to demonstrate the breadth and depth of their learning—personal meaning-making through Connections and Extensions—we use essays, projects, demonstrations, and performances. But these types of assessment activities are open to more subjective marking, that is, marking that is more interpretive and influenced by individual teacher's biases, preferences, values, and tastes. The open nature of the assessment opportunity usually results in a significant range of learning demonstrations, and those variations will require more analysis and a greater demand of teacher judgement than a traditional paper-and-pencil test might.

When we talk about maintaining objectivity, we are usually referring to our attempts to keep personal biases out of assessment so that all concerned are able to get a clear and accurate picture of a student's learning. We want to be confident that the snapshot that we provide (and so often a snapshot is all we *can* provide) is accurate. We want to know that, under similar circumstances, others would reach the same conclusions. If we can find a way to achieve the level of reliability that gives us confidence, the methods of assessment would be easy to rationalize and defend to parents, students, and administrators (and, of course, ourselves).

Herein lies the dilemma: On the one hand, we may feel reasonably confident in the reliability of grades generated by a standard, traditional, multiple-choice and short-answer exam; we may feel some additional assurance from the relative neutrality of the teachers grading them. On the other hand, we may not be satisfied that these kinds of tests encourage the kind of learning we are hoping to provide.

Students' Perceptions of Subjectivity

One way that teachers might disclose their values and biases is by letting their students know the content areas that will figure prominently on upcoming tests. It may seem trivial and just a matter of course, but any

Ideas (Basic Acceptable Response)	Connections	Extensions (Expert Response)
• Student identifies and categorizes symptoms accurately. • Student follows basic diagnostic protocol.	• Student infers cause and effect. • Student bases differential diagnoses on presented physical findings.	• Student proposes viable treatment solutions. • Student suggests potential preventive actions.

Figure 8: Suggested approaches to a nursing-school case study

information that increases students' understanding of expectations and criteria for success is a major step toward reducing subjectivity in assessment. When students know what the expectations are, they are better able to plan their learning and can base that plan on the self-assessment they're able to do as they compare their output to the stated expectations.

This may be one of the reasons that maths and sciences are so often considered to be "objective" subjects. Students are clear about what the material is they have to cover, are taught what processes to follow and what correct responses look like; most of them are actually stated in the textbook.

In fact, when science teachers take the unusual step of providing assessment opportunities that don't involve textbook-based responses, some students lose faith in the teacher's ability to assess accurately. In one such instance, after an entire term of multiple-choice unit tests, one teacher gave her nursing students a case-study-based final exam. One student was overheard to say, "I suppose she could fail me if she wants to, now that the marking will be totally subjective. I know my stuff, but I have no idea what she's looking for."

It is interesting to note that this student seemed entirely confident in her mastery of the material but wasn't at all confident about what the teacher would be using as criteria for success. Her perception of teacher subjectivity was based entirely on the fact that she did not know what the teacher's expectations were. In fact, for many assessment situations that invite the possibility of extended responses (e.g., projects, essays, presentations, performances), the criteria for success aren't shared with students until after grading has occurred. That lack of disclosure may result in students' perceptions that grading was subjective.

Consider how differently students might have reacted if the nursing instructor had shared her expectations and criteria for success beforehand through the use of a rubric. A rubric of the kind shown in Figure 8 clearly outlines the expectations the teacher has for her students' learning. Knowing what the expectations are allows students to make informed choices about

	Undeveloped <5/10	Fair 5-7/10	Good 7-8/10	Excellent 9-10/10
Skills				
Understanding				

Figure 9: Recording sheet for skills and understanding

how to study and how to approach the questions on the exam. Moreover, the students will be better equipped to self-assess based on the information provided through the rubric. When expectations and criteria are clearly set and articulated for students, they are likely to be less anxious that their work may be judged arbitrarily.

Let's fast-forward into Lesley's new semester with the senior physical education class. After distributing the grades for the basketball unit, Lesley is spending a considerable portion of her prep time explaining how she arrived at each student's mark. Each member of her class has received a slip of paper with the department's standard grading grid, and there are checkmarks in the boxes identified as Skills and Understanding (see Figure 9). The grades for Understanding are based on the results of an in-class, paper-and-pencil test on the rules of the game. The grade for Skills is based on Leslie's observations over the course of the unit and on the results of a skills circuit conducted during the last two classes.

Leslie finds that many of the students are coming to her office for an explanation of their Skills grade. From the questions her students are asking and the constructive criticism they're giving her about how they were graded, Lesley is reaching the following conclusions:

- The current grading grid is too vague to provide students with any information other than their grade.
- Aside from the grade associated with each, students seem to be unaware of the standards used to assess each skill set.
- She is spending an inordinate amount of valuable time rationalizing the grades.

At the end of the day, as she recalls the explanations she gave to her students, Lesley realizes that she had, in fact, been using her own, internalized set of criteria upon which to base her judgements and grades. Realizing how helpful it would be for them, she began the process of making those criteria explicit and accessible to her students and put them in the form of a rubric (see Figure 10).

Basketball Skill	Acceptable	Fair	Good	Excellent
Controlling Ball	• Student maintains ball control with dominant hand while stationary.	• Student maintains ball control with dominant hand while in transition from standing to jogging.	• Student maintains ball control during cross-overs from dominant to non-dominant hand. • Student dribbles across the court with head up and eyes ahead.	• Student smoothly maintains ball control through transitions in pace from standing to running with effective use of dominant and non-dominant hands.
Passing	• Student makes accurate passes to another player while both the passer and the receiver are stationary.	• Student maintains pass accuracy while the passer is stationary and the receiver is in motion.	• Student modifies pass strength to accommodate the receiver and in response to cues from the receiver and the opposition's defence.	• Student consistently completes passes on the run and creatively passes in response to changing opportunities.
Shooting	• Student uses one-handed shot with hand positioned on back of ball. • Student puts back-spin on ball.	• Student uses one-handed shot with aligned shoulder, elbow, and wrist. • Student follows through with back-spin and high arc.	• Student displays balanced body position. • Student uses legs with transfer of momentum from lower to upper body.	• Student shows smooth integration of upper and lower body movements. • Student displays efficient range of arm motion with consistent, optimal release-point. • Student focusses, ignores distractions.
Team-Playing	• Student shares court space but plays independently.	• Student performs basic manoeuvres but is often out of position. • Student contributes to an unbalanced court.	• Student responds to standard game situations using learned plays and techniques. • Student adapts positioning relative to ball and other players. • Student makes good use of peripheral vision.	• Student adapts play to new offensive and defensive actions. • Student creates opportunities for team-mates. • Student anticipates opportunities by reading the defence.

Figure 10. Rubric for assessing skill differences in basketball

If she had had the rubric to distribute before beginning the basketball unit, her students would have had a blueprint for learning and a clear indication of what the next steps toward skill improvement would entail. In addition, during their attempts to learn, students would have had an opportunity to develop self-assessment skills as they compared the level of their emerging basketball skills to the levels detailed in the rubric.

Lesley might now consider creating a similar rubric for the internalized set of criteria she normally uses for assigning grades for participation, effort, and attendance.

CONCLUSIONS

Lesley came to understand that objectivity and subjectivity have both advantages and disadvantages. Students like objective assessments because they appear not to have any teacher bias attached. The disadvantage of objective assessments is that they are designed, for the most part, to assess the lower levels of learning, whereas subjective assessments treat more complex learning. The disadvantage of subjective assessment is that many students perceive their results to be affected by factors other than what they know. Making the criteria known in advance helps to avoid many of the problems associated with subjective assessment and can even improve the resulting learning.

Five Criteria for Well-Crafted Assessments

8

JOHN O. ANDERSON

SCENARIO

Leslie Myraki and Prima Fazy teach Grade 4 classes in Maydale School and often bring their classes together so that they can engage in team teaching, particularly with their science and mathematics units. They have noticed some differences in how they assess students, and the results reported for students vary a little from one teacher to the other. Some of the differences are found in the following three situations:

1. Leslie gave a mathematics test last week and, when reviewing the results, one or two of her students pointed out that the questions were tricky. No one seemed to have a right answer, and many of the questions were on material not covered in class. Leslie thought the confusion may have been related to the use of the multiple-choice format, the first time such a format had been used with these students. Prima had similar complaints about the test she gave but thought the reason was that she had included too many simple-recall items, whereas the unit had been on problem identification in word problems in mathematics.

2. When checking her own students' portfolios, Leslie normally included a lot of comments about how they should change their work in order to improve, while Prima tended to write encouraging remarks of a general nature on her students' portfolios. Furthermore, when they assessed each others' student portfolios, they would often give students different grades.

3. The students of both teachers have occasionally complained that one teacher "marked harder" than the other. The gist of the comments was: "I get better marks from Ms. Fazy than from Mr. Myraki."

Students deserve fair and consistent assessment of their learning and achievements. How can we make this happen?

WHAT YOU WILL LEARN IN THIS ESSAY

- that evaluation practice itself can be evaluated in order to insure that it is working well;
- that assessment practice can be monitored in relation to fairness, relevance, accuracy, consistency, and sustainability (FRACS).

DISCUSSION

Leslie and Prima decide to read up on assessment as it is currently being practised and share notes with each other. They found that:

- Assessing students has several recognized purposes, the two most common of which are: (1) feedback to each student and to the teacher on the achievement status on the several learning dimensions with which they are engaged, not only curricular areas such as reading, writing, mathematics, science, and social studies but also other areas such as responsibility and social skills; (2) reporting achievement and progress to students and parents.
- Classroom assessment requires the collection of information about students. The information often takes the form of products such as written texts, projects, tests, and portfolios, but it may also include observations in various others settings, such as social interactions, independent work, or physical activities.
- The teacher must collect and make meaning of a broad spectrum of information about each student's achievement of learning goals of schooling, a complex task. This volume provides guidelines and procedures for how to develop assessment procedures that yield relevant information about student achievement, and how to develop and use rubrics to make judgements about the quality of student performance and the reporting achievement results. The five-point FRACS framework is helpful for facing this challenge.

Fairness

Every student should experience equal assessment treatment. In the contemporary diverse classroom, this means that the teacher must design different methods of assessment for different students and at the same time balance results across the class to yield grades that fairly represent student achievement.

To achieve this in the classroom, teachers need to set reasonable expectations—achievable but not constraining—and explain them fully to each student.

One of the great benefits of team teaching for Leslie and Prima is that they are often able to discuss the learning goals and achievement expectations they have for their students. They extend these discussions to include the students themselves to insure that they understand the directions of their learning and that they own their learning. The identification and description of the goals for their students demand wise professional judgement that is based upon a comprehensive understanding of the curriculum and the learning capacities of their students. This openness to discussion facilitates fairness in Leslie's and Prima's assessment practice; it brings students and professional judgement into the centre of the conversation.

Leslie and Prima are careful to make their students aware of their expectations and how they will go about assessing their achievements. They use rubrics to do this because the rubrics are designed to help students understand and cogently discuss and negotiate their own goals, expectations, and assessment methods as part of their learning. But the teacher should describe the boundaries within which students can map their learning outcomes. Teachers may want to describe the minimal levels of competency expected but at the same time be clear that these levels are not the standard or the ceiling of possible accomplishment.

Students should always feel comfortable asking why. Why are we doing this? is a strong assessment question. The teacher should have answers that she or he can not only live with but also discuss with colleagues, students, and parents. If students feel comfortable asking why and understand the reasons behind assessment practices in the classroom, the benefits will be dual: assessment and learning. Teachers need to listen carefully to the answers when they ask why. Teachers need to keep an index of fairness and the extent of student understanding of any assessment practice, and this could be based on the answers that students give when asked, Why are we doing this?

Relevance

Assessments should be relevant to the learning goals of the curriculum. While not every single learning outcome of most curricula needs to be assessed, a sample of outcomes that have a solid relationship to the curriculum as a whole could be selected. They should represent the curriculum, not be chosen just for their ease of assessment. As with all aspects of assessment, in order to make wise choices about what learning outcomes to target for classroom assessment, teachers need to rely on sound professional knowledge of curriculum and of students. Discussions with colleagues can help to insure that the outcomes chosen indeed reflect the important elements of the curriculum.

Accuracy

There are at least two interrelated aspects of accuracy in classroom assessment. One is the extent to which the task asked of students is directly related to the learning goal that is being assessed. For example, let's assume that a teacher wants to assess student understanding of narrative as an element of expression. This may be assessed through story-telling (live presentation to peers), writing a narrative account, writing and story-telling in combination, or perhaps creating and producing a play. There are many specifics involved in such tasks (e.g., choice of topics, length, and format), but the point is that there are many ways in which understanding of narrative can be assessed, and the teacher needs to evaluate which task(s) best reflect(s) the expectations associated with the learning target.

Discussion with colleagues is one of the best ways to find the tasks that accurately tap into student's abilities in relation to the desired learning outcomes. In developing assessment procedures and materials, teachers need to clearly link the tasks and grading criteria (the rubrics) to the learning outcomes under assessment. Teachers should also explicitly discuss with students the purpose, form, and grading of assessment so that each and every one of them clearly understands what is expected. Students are generally good critics of the accuracy of classroom assessment practice and if given the opportunity will give their views openly.

Secondly, the teacher's evaluation of a student (an evaluative comment, category label, grade, or mark) should accurately reflect the level that the student has achieved. The evaluation should be based solely on the performance of the student on the specific task chosen. The ICE model (see Introduction) and specially constructed rubrics are both excellent frameworks that can help teachers keep assessment and evaluation of student achievement clearly focussed on learning targets.

Consistency

The consistency of teachers' assessment practice should focus on both how each student is treated and on judgement from one assessment occasion to another.

Consistency among students is a basic element of fairness, and it will be enhanced if all students clearly understand the assessment tasks in the same way. This can be a particular challenge for teachers in classrooms with diverse groups of students, some of whom have difficulties in English (as assessment is generally language-based, whether it be oral or written). Maintaining consistency is a challenge as well when it is necessary that assessment take on different forms for different students. For example, a teacher might be interested in assessing students' understandings of field ecosystems using a learning portfolio. Students might create highly divergent kinds of collections varying from collections of field samples, video images, written reports, collections of audio-taped interviews and bird songs, or other materials. Well-structured task descriptions and rubrics are invaluable in helping keep the assessment focussed on the underlying learning goals, regardless of the specifics of student performance and production.

Sustainability

Teaching is a complex and difficult endeavour, and assessment is but one of the many responsibilities that teachers undertake. Assessment has to be continually in operation in the classroom, and it needs to be sustainable. Indeed, if sustainability fails, all else is jeopardized. A teacher can devote only so much time to classroom assessment and so must insure that he or she works efficiently at sustaining assessment.

Teachers need to carefully select only those learning outcomes that are most important within a given curriculum. They need to use assessment formats that are efficient, relevant, accurate and at the same time can be implemented consistently.

CONCLUSIONS

The first situation described at the beginning of this essay involved the math test in which students found some of the test items tricky. And they perceived the test to have been unfair, in that the test items seemed unrelated to what they had been doing in math during the previous few weeks. Some students thought that a test featuring recall was irrelevant, since problem-solving had been the focus of math classes over the previous weeks.

After hearing her students' comments, Leslie thought seriously about the relationship between what was being asked of students in a multiple-choice format (single-solution responses) and the work the students had been doing. In class, Leslie had been asking students to identify problem issues and come up with a variety of possible solutions before testing them out, a unique approach to solving problems. After discussing this with Prima, she decided that they should reconsider how well the multiple-choice format meets their assessment needs in mathematics problem-solving specifically. They concluded that, if in the future they chose to use an assessment format that was new to students (such as multiple-choice, and particularly if it were to count toward final grades), they should introduce the new format to the students well ahead of time. Thus, the assessment would be about mathematics and not adapting to new formats. Perhaps the test items were not accurate representations of the curriculum. The new assessment format (in this case multiple-choice) may have skewed students' perceptions of what the tests were about to the point that they were not focussed on the mathematics involved.

The second situation described how two teachers might assess student portfolios in very different ways. Portfolios are useful in encouraging students to take ownership of their own learning and to demonstrate their learning accomplishments in their own ways. Leslie provided feedback to students to help them improve performance on important targets and skills, and this is certainly a valid assessment activity. Prima gave encouraging comments to help keep students engaged in portfolio development. This, too, particularly when coupled with diagnostic feedback, was a valid assessment activity.

The grading of portfolios, because of their individual character, will always introduce issues of consistency in relation to equity among students. However, teachers can use various techniques to enhance consistency in grading; clear rubrics, for example, would illustrate clearly what criteria were being used and what students should aim for in their work.

The third situation described students who voiced their concerns about assessment practices and evaluation standards of their team teachers: the two teachers grade differently. This is clearly an issue of perceived inconsistency and unfairness, not necessarily real. Prima took these comments seriously; she wanted to insure that her students were treated equitably regardless of which teacher graded their work. As a first step, she discussed their marking styles and expectations with Leslie. The discussion was centred on the rubrics they had developed for grading student work and how they might each evaluate the same samples of student work. They finished by developing a small experiment to evaluate the consistency of their grading practices. They both graded the same set of student papers to first of all check whether the student comments were warranted and then to devise how they could establish and maintain consistent standards and grading in their assessment practice.

They always kept uppermost in their minds throughout their experiment the five-point framework for evaluating assessment practice because it is based on open, honest, and constant observation and reflection on their own practice. The believed that these five points would pave the way to sound assessment in their classroom. The comfort level with any teacher's assessment practices can be enhanced through constant dialogue with colleagues, students, and parents.

Choosing among Various Models of Learning and Assessment 9

MARK LEE

SCENARIO

Amelia Thesiger has taught high school for three years and is now interested in examining how she assesses students, aligns her instruction and assessment practices, and identifies the assumptions and beliefs she holds that underpin these practices.

She majored in psychology as an undergraduate arts student and wrote a thesis on learning processes in young children as a graduate student. During her year studying in a faculty of education, she was disappointed in the lack of depth and integration of learning theory that was presented in her classes. In particular, she remembers one professor of instructional design who believed that students should construct their own learnings. While he adopted an appropriate instructional style that supported this belief, he assessed students only on their recollection of relevant concepts taught in class.

So, now that Amelia has a couple of teaching years under her belt, she feels that she can turn her attention to comparing her own observation of student learning and assessment to models she might find in educational literature. Recently, presenters of professional development seminars at her school have recommended that teachers follow a problem-based curriculum that focusses on the cognitive skills of students and measures their cognitive growth. However, Amelia feels that most of these seminars do not clearly outline particular models; rather, they allude to such models in only a general way.

She feels that an explicit description of the various models of student learning and assessments would help clarify her thinking. As things stand, she often feels pulled between wanting to devise assessments that show how students' thinking has developed (a cognitive-constructivist approach) and meeting the reporting needs of the school. These reporting needs usually require that teachers merely add up the overall number of facts, concepts, and procedures that students remember from their lessons and record them on reports (a behaviourist model of learning). Amelia's dilemma is basically this: How can she reconcile administrative requirements for reporting with the need to assess in-depth student learning?

WHAT YOU WILL LEARN IN THIS ESSAY

- that several models of student learning have been developed, and they differ in their assumptions about the nature of learning and knowledge;
- that the assessment rubrics that logically flow from various learning models differ;
- that there are sources of information that can be used in making judgements about changes in assessment practice.

DISCUSSION

Amelia begins her examination with a look at several articles and books that outline various models of student learning. She makes the following notes:

- Both the cognitive theory and the constructivist theory of learning suggest that students process information to generate mental models, or schema, that provide them with the ability to remember information, perform tasks, and solve problems.
- Some features of these schema are both explicit and implicit and difficult for students to articulate, for example, like trying to explain to a non-swimmer the complicated sequence in moving arms, legs, and head in the front crawl.
- Learning occurs when schema are created within the brain.
- Schema become integrated and more complex as learning proceeds.
- As pre-existing cognitive schema become integrated with new ones, this learning involves the use of prior experience and understandings.

Proponents of the cognitive learning model believe that experience and reflection on experience are necessary elements of the learning process. By reflecting, students construct new knowledge within their own learning context.

Amelia's search causes her to remember a group of international students she taught in a core-area urban school. She remembers the difficulties that several Chinese and Middle-Eastern students had when they were confronted with North American concepts and practices. In particular, some students had difficulty completing work as individuals rather than as part of a group. Some students had difficulty with math problems in which typical

North American concepts were featured, such as a snow bank or a suburban back yard. Students often reformulated problems according to concepts and ideas that were familiar to them.

Amelia's summary of the notes she took from the literature makes the following points:

- Cognitive and constructivist instructional practices typically place the student at the centre of his or her learning and encourage independent thinking.
- Teachers need to present information and problem-solving activities to students and invite them to generate their own understanding of the problems and create their own solutions using their prior understanding.

The student-centred model of instruction naturally leads teachers to include topics and subjects that students are interested in and feel motivated to learn about (as students tend to be more interested in things that they might have already been motivated to look at).

Educators who hold cognitive-constructivist beliefs about student learning appreciate the individual and complex nature of each student's learning. Consequently, they typically employ assessments that involve student input and that attempt to acknowledge the unique nature of each student's learning. Teachers of this ilk often coordinate student-led assessment sessions (particularly of their portfolios) to trace the process of student learning. As well, they often pursue the quality of student learning as a measure of schema development, using tools that get at the extent to which students have integrated their prior learning with current learning or have transferred their learning in one area to another.

Proponents of social constructivism, too, stress the importance of prior knowledge and experience in students' learning. However, they also emphasize the central role of peers and teachers and of practice within specific current contexts to increase knowledge. The construction of knowledge is understood to occur when motivated learners interact with others and with the learning environment. This aspect of the learning process as understood within the model of social constructivism is referred to as "situated cognition."

Social constructivists (and many cognitive constructivists) understand the process of learning on a continuum between novice and expert, where the novice has concrete, factual knowledge and the expert has complex, abstract knowledge. As students construct meaning for themselves, their new learning will be different from that exhibited by the expert.

	Level 1	Level 2	Level 3	Level 4
Thesis	Student presents a simple (one-point) thesis statement.	Student presents a (one-point) thesis statement that is supported by literature.	Student presents a thesis statement that contains two central points and is supported by literature.	Student presents a thesis statement containing three or more central points and is supported by literature.
Writing Style	Student makes 4 or more grammar errors (described in class).	Student makes 3 grammar errors.	Student consistently makes only 2 grammar errors.	Student consistently makes 1 or no grammar errors.
Research	Student shows thorough use of at least 5 sources in their papers (a minimum of 2 quotes per source).	Student shows thorough use of 8 sources in their papers (a minimum of 3 quotes per source).	Student shows thorough use of 10 sources in their papers (4 quotes per source).	Student shows a thorough use of at least 12 sources in their papers (4 quotes per source).
Presentation	Student follows at least 2 of the 8 presentation rules described by the teacher in class .	Student follows at least 4 of the 8 presentation rules described by the teacher in class.	Student follows at least 6 of the 8 presentation rules described by the teacher in class.	Student follows all of the 8 presentation rules described by the teacher in class.

Figure 11. A rubric designed for grading a history essay that follows the behaviourist model of learning

Amelia recalls another incident that applies to what she is reading. It is a set of lessons on logic and argument construction that she conducted with her history class earlier in the year. An initial chalk-and-talk lesson on the components of arguments inspired little interest (or achievement on a class quiz on the topic). However, when she gave quizzes and assigned short essays about the arguments presented in a series of classroom debates, Amelia found that her students came to understand the notion of argument in increasingly sophisticated ways. Many students offered complex explanations about the concept on the term exam that drew on ideas not directly covered in classroom handouts.

Proponents of behaviourist theories of learning, by contrast, hold that learning results from action of the environment on the learner. Behaviourists do not examine how student learning occurs but are, rather, focussed on ways that students can be taught to behave in order to complete certain tasks (e.g., remembering facts or performing the correct procedures to complete such tasks). According to this theory, the student is seen as a vessel to be filled with information, factual and procedural. Behaviourists tend to view knowledge quantitatively, that is, as information that can be directly transmitted to students through instruction. Furthermore, behaviourists typically believe in teacher-centred classroom activities and the use of much classroom material (e.g., texts, articles) that are to be absorbed directly by students. Assessments are typically designed to measure student recall of facts and procedures.

Amelia finds the description of these models of learning, knowledge, and instruction interesting but wonders about the ways that they might translate into assessment tools. She decides to do a little experiment; she sketches out a mock assessment in the form of a four-level rubric for a history essay that she is planning to assign to a group of Grade 12 students the following week (see Figures 11 and 12).

After sketching out these two mock rubrics, Amelia muses that, if she wanted to align her rubrics with the tenets of social constructivist theory, she would need to add elements that looked at the quality of student interaction with other students and with other features of the environment.

CONCLUSIONS

Amelia will be mindful of her assumptions about student learning as she makes adjustments to her teaching practice. In considering the results of her exploration, she realizes three important things. First, she is not interested in adopting only one model of assessment for all situations in the classroom. For example, there are learning situations where it is highly appropriate to examine the number of facts that a student has gathered rather than the

	Level 1	Level 2	Level 3	Level 4
Thesis	Student presents a thesis statement.	Student presents a thesis statement that is logically connected to the main argument in the paper. The relevance of this thesis to the student's own interests and experience is made clear in a short rationale.	Student presents a thesis statement and argument that are well supported by connections to relevant literature.	Student presents a well-researched and well-supported argument in the paper that is connected to learning outside of the subject area or to an area relevant to the student's life.
Writing style	Student's writing style does not interfere with comprehension of the central argument or supporting evidence in the paper.	Student has chosen relevant vocabulary to help make the argument clear.	Student has chosen relevant vocabulary and has made an effort to organize his or her paper in a way that facilitates the reader's comprehension.	Student has chosen advanced methods (poems, prose) that support the organization of the paper and facilitates reader comprehension.
Research	Student shows mastery of relevant sources in the papers.	Student demonstrates integration of source materials to support the main argument.	Student illustrates how an integrated understanding of source materials is connected to the rationale.	Student's integration of research materials leads naturally to discussion of a significant or novel issue that flows from the argument presented in the paper.
Presentation	Student uses appropriate methods of presentation in the paper.	Student uses pictures and formatting to support the argument presented in the paper.	Student presents the paper in a way that helps the reader understand how the central argument of the paper is connected to the rationale for choosing the topic.	Student presents a paper in which a discussion of some significant or novel issue flows from the argument presented in the paper.

Figure 12. A rubric designed for grading a history essay that follows a cognitive-constructivist model of learning

depth of learning that a student has demonstrated. Indeed, it is important to combine features of the two models; in this way, no dimension of student learning is left out of the assessment mix.

Second, there are underlying conceptions of learning and knowledge that are critical to her instructional design. For instance, if a more social-constructivist than cognitive-constructivist model of learning is presumed, then it might be necessary to enhance interaction among class members (group learning) or increase the use of older peer mentors.

Third, there is a need to align her conceptions of knowledge and learning with her instruction and assessment practices.

Assessing for Learning and Assessment of Learning 10

ROBERT J. WILSON

SCENARIO

Principal Sheyla Murray, recently back from a district-wide meeting, has informed her staff that it will now be district policy to assess students on all their work using a standard rubric. This rubric is to be used not only in class but also on report cards and on provincial results, so that parents and others will be able to compare achievement from report to report.

Angela Tripp tries this out with her Grade 7 class and finds real difficulty distinguishing between phrases on the rubric like "frequently makes errors" and "seldom makes errors" in many of the activities she has her class do. When she focusses on the task of helping her students become self-evaluators, it is even more clear that these distinctions are hard to explain. Her dilemma is how to adhere to her principal's wishes while still focussing on her students' learning and growth.

WHAT YOU WILL LEARN IN THIS ESSAY

- what the differences are between formative and summative assessment and why they are important;
- how the two systems can be reconciled and made to fit into a plan;
- why common reporting is not the same as common assessment;
- what makes for sound classroom assessment and sound external assessment, and how they fit together.

DISCUSSION

We do assessments in order to make some decisions: for example, enter marks into a recording book; and, in Angela's case, have students maintain a portfolio of work to show their parents on conference day.

One important way for teachers to think about the assessments they design for themselves and their students is that helping students learn is the primary goal. The assessments should both inform students about what they are accomplishing and point the way to what they might do next. The assessments should also tell the teacher about what to teach next, what to review, and what to teach over again. And involving students in this kind of assessment can go a long way to help them become self-assessors. Assessment done according to these guidelines is called "formative assessment."

Often, formative assessment occurs "on the run." While Angela is doing something else, she notices that Alain is struggling over punctuation, especially the use of commas, or that Olympia has finished her project—satisfactorily in her mind—and is now looking for something else to do. (Olympia often thinks that the purpose of schoolwork is to get it finished, not necessarily to get it right. A little visit by the teacher to Olympia's work station and a pointed question or two might show her that there might be more to be learned from the activity.)

Alain might be helped by some instruction on how pairs of commas are used to set off non-essential phrases. So Angela has him read out the sentence that is giving him problems: "Billy and his horse but not the dog galloped down the trail to the shed."

"Notice how you changed your voice when you were part way through the sentence. Where was that, Alain?"

He reads it out loud again. "I sort of stopped after horse."

"And when did you pick it up again?"

"After 'dog.'"

"Right. How does it help to put commas around that phrase?"

"I guess it tells the reader to do what I did."

"Good thinking! Now look through the rest of your story to see if there are other places where the same rule would apply."

This kind of formative assessment may not require careful planning, but it certainly involves creativity; in fact, it most often occurs spontaneously in the day-to-day activity. These spontaneous observations are frequently cited by teachers as the most important assessments they ever make; indeed, they are the most informative way of assessing the learning that is going on in their classrooms.

Rubrics, too, can be used for assessment for learning, when it becomes important to Angela that her students know two things: (1) what the expectations are for both her and her students; and (2) what good work looks like. Figure 13 is an example of a rubric that she and her class created for an expository writing assignment.

Angela sometimes has her students advise her about what should go into the rubric (although she frequently has to amalgamate their suggestions when assembling the final format). By taking the time to get her students' advice, she ensures that both she and her students know what a good job looks like and what it would take to make it better.

	Ideas	Connections	Extensions
Legibility	Letters and words are recognizable.	The process of making final drafts from rough drafts shows attention to legibility.	The product includes displays of materials, drawings, or tables.
Sentence Structure	Sentences begin with capitals and end with periods or question marks.	Sentences are linked.	Sentence structure is varied throughout to create effects on reader.
Planning	Research is evident; ideas are listed.	Ideas are ordered and sources identified.	Ideas are selected with needs of reader in mind.
Audience	Readers are identified.	Diction is appropriate to the background of the audience.	Writing invites audience involvement in the ideas.

Figure 13. An ICE rubric created by a teacher and her students for assessing expository writing assignment

For this assignment (i.e., when students are asked to advise her), the class first discusses what elements they think would be important to consider. They (and Angela) agree that legibility, sentence structure, and planning are important; Angela also wanted research to be a big part of the assignment, and she thought consideration of audience would be important. Sometimes the elements do not appear in the exact form that Angela would like, but she frequently allows her students to use labels that are meaningful to them.

They then apply the ICE model to the elements. The ICE model allows the students and Angela to show what the learnings would look like as it got more complex. Ideas are the building blocks of learning; they are the bits and pieces that are necessary. In this project, the ideas include: the letters and words used in writing; appropriate sentence structure and format; the concepts gleaned from the research; and knowledge of who the audience will be. Connections can be of two types: (1) within the work itself (sentences linked together in coherent order); and, (2) within the knowledge of an individual person or among several people (the writer writes with an audience in mind). Extensions occur when the writer goes beyond what is required and produces something that truly shines.

When Angela looks at the rubrics that Sheyla has brought back from her meeting (see Figure 14), she finds them less than useful in the context of her own teaching.

Angela concludes that there could be a place for reporting to students and their parents in the way the district requires. That is, summative assessments (the name we give to assessments that occur at the end of some process)

	Level 1	Level 2	Level 3	Level 4
Reasoning		**The student reasons:**		
	with assistance using a few simple ideas inconsistently and with limited understanding	with limited assistance using a variety of simple and related ideas consistently and with limited understanding	independently using ideas of some complexity consistently and with general understanding	independently using complex ideas consistently and with thorough understanding
Communication		**The student communicates:**		
	with assistance but not clearly for a limited range of simple purposes with a limited range of simple forms	independently with some clarity and some precision for a variety of simple purposes with several different forms	independently clearly and precisely for specific purposes with a variety of forms	independently clearly, precisely, and confidently for a wide variety of purposes and in a wide variety of contexts with a wide range of complex forms
Organization of Ideas		**The student organizes:**		
	with assistance but not completely for a limited range of simple purposes	independently in a mechanical and sequential way for a variety of simple purposes	independently appropriately and logically for specific purposes	independently appropriately and in complex and logical ways for a wide variety of purposes and in a wide variety of contexts
Application of Language Conventions (spelling, grammar, punctuation, and style)		**The student applies conventions:**		
	with assistance using a few of the conventions studied with several major errors and/or omissions	with limited assistance using at least half of the conventions studied with several minor errors and/or omissions	independently using most of the conventions studied with a few minor errors and/or omissions	independently using all the conventions studied, in a wide variety of contexts with practically no minor errors and/or omissions

Figure 14. Achievement levels in language, Grades 1-8, Province of Ontario (from OME, 2004, 12-13)

might be useful (assessment *of* learning); formative assessment would be more useful in aiding learning (assessment *for* learning).

Angela uses the package of materials her students keep in their portfolios to assess the changes and developments they have made. When parents visit, they, too, appreciate seeing samples of work that their children have done, especially when there are samples of the same activity done at different times.

Angela knows that her students' parents wish to have more normative, comparative data as well as demonstrations of what they have been doing in school. It is here that the summary rubrics have their place. They are laden with evaluative words, which need translation (e.g., What are "minor errors"? What does "with limited assistance" mean? What are "ideas of some complexity" for a Grade 7 student?). Angela is able to translate these judgements into language that indicates the degree to which Alain's and Olympia's achievements are typical for their grade. Moreover, she is able to provide parents with examples that illustrate these rather abstract statements.

It is very important to Angela that students produce work that is complex and shows the processes they are using. She needs products from her learners, pieces of evidence that show her how they went about what they were doing, why they did it the way they did, where they need help, and what they can do to extend their learning. She does not need the same piece of work from each of her learners; in fact, it is better if each one produces work that shows their individual approaches to learning. Her own rubrics are useful because they list the criteria that everyone in the class agrees to; they do not require that all students do the same exercises in the same way.

Flexibility and individuality are not as easily achieved when comparisons among learners or comparisons of learners to formal standards are desired (as they are in the Ministry's scheme). Such comparisons are less than helpful to Angela in planning what Olympia should be working on next in mathematics, but they do answer the question Olympia's parents have about her progress in the context of her age and grade level.

CONCLUSIONS

Angela uses her own, customized assessment system most of the time. She wants to help her students learn and be able to monitor themselves while they are learning. Near reporting times, she accommodates the Ministry's needs by filling in the standard form, placing it in each student's display portfolio, which parents will see, and working hard at translating the jargon into meaningful terms.

II School Practices

Teachers face many dilemmas, not so much in carrying out their own practices but, more, in making their practices fit with school demands. For example, every school is likely to have policies surrounding reporting and accumulating information for that reporting. Secondary schools in particular may require that all students in a particular course with multiple sections undergo the same assessments. This policy creates a dilemma: What if a student is absent from these mandated common assessments? The first two essays in this section look at this type of dilemma.

Most schools today attempt to involve their teachers in building their policies and practices. This approach makes sense, especially if the goal is to make a sound policy approach that everyone can buy into. Saying that collaboration and cooperation are essential and achieving collaboration and cooperation, however, are two different things. The next three chapters in this section provide detailed information on how to say it as well as achieve it.

Making Different Tests Equivalent

11

SUE FOSTATY YOUNG

SCENARIO

In an effort to eliminate scheduling conflicts for students, the Regional District School Board has decided to adopt a new exam schedule. Traditionally, all students in a given course wrote the final exam at the same time. However, the schedule resulted in double bookings for a significant number of students, and new exam times had to be created for these double-booked students. The proposed new schedule eliminates the possibility of scheduling conflicts by having all students in Period 1 write their exams on Day 1, all students in Period 2 write on Day 2, and so on. That proposal, of course, means that some students in a given course would write on Day 1 while others would have to wait until Day 4, and teachers would need to provide a different version of the exam for each exam day. Principals in the region assure their staff members that the problems associated with having several versions of the same exam could be minimized through some up-front, collaborative planning and question-banking. Other principals are not so sure.

WHAT YOU WILL LEARN IN THIS ESSAY

- how to make different versions of the same test equal through collaborative planning, and employing tables of specification, test-question banks, and post-test analysis and equating;
- how to minimize the problems of using several versions of a test to generate grades for reporting.

DISCUSSION

When providing scores for purposes of record-keeping and documenting learning achievement at the administrative level, teachers generally make an assumption that the scores will be used to compare the relative standing of students one to another. The inferences and comparisons made among various students' results are based on an assumption that the grades are comparable—

that they are generated by assessing comparable activities and similar opportunities, and then subjected to identical criteria for success. When different tests, different conditions, and different criteria are used to generate scores, the accuracy of subsequent comparisons is compromised. The challenge is to create assessment opportunities—in this case final exams—that are similar enough to be considered fair and comparable while, at the same time, being different enough so that they minimize the potential for answer-sharing among the test-takers. How one would make sure that different tests are comparable is a technical process. It is described in detail under the next four headings.

Minimizing the Problems

In their attempt to provide each set of students with similar opportunities for comparable demonstrations of learning, teachers need to ensure that the quality of the exams remains constant from class to class, term to term, and year to year. Some teachers and department heads will opt for a repeating series of exams, rotating through them every three or four terms. Others will create a new exam for each testing period. The former option could result in answer-sharing among students who discover the pattern, and the latter attempts to eliminate the effects of sharing. Both methods could result in fluctuating test quality and changes in content-focus.

One tool for constructing tests that attempts to address both these issues is the table of specifications. These tables serve to outline curriculum content areas and provide opportunities for demonstrations of different levels of learning and the relative weighting of each component as part of the final exam. The process is valuable for four reasons:

1. It provides an opportunity for teachers to share their beliefs and values about course content and learning.
2. It helps foster collaboration among members of the teaching department.
3. It provides an explicit guide for the content-focus and grade-weights for the exams.
4. It can be shared with students for use as a study guide.

To develop a table of specifications as an exam guide, teachers need to agree on: the curriculum content areas to be included on the final exam; the relative grade-weight contribution of each content area on the exam; the level of learning to be demonstrated in each content area; and the relative grade-weight contribution of each type of learning to the overall exam.

	Ideas	Connections	Extensions	Totals
Content Area 1				20%
Content Area 2				30%
Content Area 3				15%
Content Area 4				10%
Content Area 5				10%
Content Area 6				15%
Totals				**100%**

Figure 15. Template of table of specification using the ICE model

Agreeing on the Content to be Covered

Final-exam questions should address the main topics in a course of study and focus on the content areas most strongly related to the primary learning outcomes as stated in the course curriculum. It is very likely that there will be too many topics to include in the test, so teachers need to be selective. As a matter of course, a review of the units of study and their sub-topics usually yield the list of content or topic highlights to be included, and each teacher is likely to have opinions about which content areas are of greatest, and least, importance.

Determining Grade-Weights

Once the areas of content have been selected, teachers must agree on the relative importance of each area and the prominence of each within the test. A department may decide to adopt a specific formula for final exams, say, having Content Area 1 contributing 20 percent of the grade-weight, Content Area 2 contributing 30 percent of the grade-weight, and so on (see Figure 15).

Level of Learning

Once teachers have agreed on the content-focus of the exam, the next critical step is that they agree upon the level of learning to be assessed in each content area. Is it the teacher's intention to focus the assessment on students' grasp of the fundamental elements such as definitions, introductory concepts, and facts? Or is the exam intended, instead, as an exercise in critical thinking for students, as a way for them to demonstrate facility with concepts, applying them in novel ways and using them to solve abstract problems? Is the intention to offer an opportunity for students to demonstrate learning at a number of levels?

	Ideas	Connections	Extensions	Totals
Content Area 1	5	5	10	20%
Content Area 2		15	15	30%
Content Area 3	10	5		15%
Content Area 4		5	5	10%
Content Area 5		10		10%
Content Area 6	5		10	15%
Totals	**20%**	**40%**	**40%**	**100%**

Figure 16. Partially completed table of specifications using the ICE model

It may well be that the answers to these questions will vary by content areas. Using the ICE model as a framework, some teachers might emphasize the Ideas level in some content and Connections categories and Extensions in others. The department might create a table of specifications that looks something like that shown in Figure 16.

Relative Grade-Weight Contribution

Once they have constructed the initial table of specifications, teachers can review it critically to ensure that the proposed makeup of the exam is an accurate reflection of the opportunities that the examiners and/or teachers hope to provide for their students. In the scenario presented in this essay, the teachers wanted to ensure a high degree of competence and so wanted to create a test that was skewed toward Connection and Extensions levels of learning in the ICE model. In this test, students with only basic knowledge of the course material would be unlikely to pass, and only those with competent or expert facility would be likely to do well.

It often happens that teachers agree on the content to be tested but leave the weightings for assessment of the level of learning undiscussed. Figure 17 shows how completing a full table of specifications can be time effective. This scale was generated as a result of the review of an already existing exam for the same unit of study. Notice the discrepancies in the values associated with each of the levels of learning. Notice, too, that this exam, with the same course content as shown in Figure 16, has an entirely different focus. While the grade-weight totals for each content area are identical in both tables, there is a significant difference in the type of learning being tested by each of the exams. Figure 17 shows the outline for a test that is heavily skewed toward Ideas- and Connections-level learning; the exam tests course fundamentals, fact acquisition, and meaning-making, with comparably fewer opportunities for students to demonstrate learning at the Extensions level.

	Ideas	Connections	Extensions	Totals
Content Area 1	10	10		20%
Content Area 2	10	15	5	30%
Content Area 3	10	5		15%
Content Area 4		5	5	10%
Content Area 5		5	5	10%
Content Area 6	10	5		15%
Totals	**40%**	**45%**	**15%**	**100%**

Figure 17. Final table of specifications (after examination is complete) using the ICE model

Students with even basic knowledge and understanding of the course material are likely to do well on this test, while those who have mastered the material to a higher level will have an opportunity to demonstrate that the level of expertise required to do well on this test is not what the teachers had intended when they created their target table of specifications. All the content areas are the same as in Figure 16, and all their row totals are identical, but the exams generated through the use of each will be very different, as will the resulting grades.

Creating Balanced Questions and Establishing a Question-Bank

A good place to begin creating a question-bank is with old exams, Internet test sites, and teacher-resource materials. First sort the questions into Ideas, Connections, and Extensions categories. Questions that restrict responses to a reiteration of facts, recall of basic information, or recognition of fundamentals are ideal for assessing Ideas-level learning. These questions are often closed, in that they limit responses rather than encourage elaboration. Some potential question starters for Ideas-level responses are:

List the...

Define...

Who was...

Paraphrase the...

Identify...

Fill-in-the-blank, short-answer, and multiple-choice questions all can be as effective in eliciting Ideas-level responses as the question starters listed above. Review multiple-choice questions critically; any that specifically limit responses to knowledge of facts, vocabulary, and fundamentals should be categorized as Ideas-type questions.

Next add questions that require students to explain relationships among various elements of the course content or that relate the course material in a meaningful way to their experience outside of class. These are Connections-level questions. For example:

> Compare________to________
>
> Estimate…
>
> Explain the relationship between…
>
> How does________affect________
>
> Using an example from your own experience, show how...

While multiple-choice, short-answer, and true/false questions can be used to assess learning at the Connections level, they must be skilfully crafted to be effective. Questions that get at cause/effect relationships or those that require the student to make inferences and deductions are some examples of Connections-type questions.

It may be tempting to immediately categorize complex questions as either Connections- or Extensions-type questions simply because of their structure. Instead, pay attention to the demonstrations of learning that they invite. The critical question to ask is, Does this question promote learning? If the answer is in the affirmative, categorize it appropriately and move on; if it's the latter, reformulate the question, categorize it, and then move on.

Multiple-choice, fill-in-the-blank, true/false, and short-answer questions are all good for Ideas and Connections, but they are inappropriate as Extensions-type questions. They restrict responses and do not provide students the opportunity to demonstrate their full range of learning. Some Extension-type questions include:

> State and support your opinion on …
>
> Predict how …
>
> Propose an alternative to …
>
> What are the implications of …

While questions like those listed above may invite extended responses, they needn't (and shouldn't) exclude responses at either the Ideas or the Connections level. In fact, teachers can (and should) formulate essay-type exam questions in such a way that they will be accessible to all students and extendable by some. An example is in the question starter, Explain the relationship between … A response at the Ideas level will include a list of the

Ideas	Connections	Extensions
• Student uses accurate definitions and uses of terms, vocabulary, and elemental concepts correctly. • Student reiterates facts.	• Student clearly indicates and articulates the relationships among concepts. • Student shows evidence of understanding of learning in relation to real-life experience • Student shows evidence of meaning-making.	• Student is able to answer hypothetical questions and make predictions based on what was learned. • Student uses learning in a novel way, different from the initial learning situation.

Figure 18. Basic rubric for developing an answer key using the ICE model

characteristics of each of the two elements under comparison. A response at the Connections level will include the characteristics of both elements, and it will outline the existing relationship. A response at the Extensions level will include as well the implications of the relationships perhaps to future practice or developments. These kinds of questions are posed in such a way as to be accessible to all, and students can demonstrate their learning at whatever level it happens to be.

As teachers review past exams, on-line test sites, and as they locate other teacher-resource materials and sort questions by content area and ICE category, they will begin to accumulate a question-bank. When it comes time to construct the exam, all they need to do is select the appropriate number and type of questions (Ideas, Connections, and Extensions) for each content area. And they will find it easy to continue adding categorized questions to the question-bank.

Creating the Answer-Key Rubric

For each exam question that might elicit a range of responses from wonderfully insightful to woefully lacking, teachers need to be equipped with an answer key. Because ICE rubrics themselves are comprehensive, qualitative descriptions of the three levels of progressively deeper learning, they can be particularly useful in the development of answer keys (see Figure 18).

Each rubric should be made question-specific, and the basic format should remain consistent across questions and be reflective of the characteristics of learning at each of the three ICE levels. Grade-values and ranges associated with each answer type should be agreed upon before marking begins; inter-rater reliability can easily be tested with blind reviews.

CONCLUSIONS

The degree to which tests and their results are equal depends on the manner in which they are constructed. To ensure comparability, teachers need to discuss and collaborate about the blueprints used to create them; tables of specification are the best tool, as they ensure that the same content will appear on all tests and that the level of learning tested is similar. To do this requires creating or selecting items at different levels as well. The scoring of subjective items, a major source of differences in marking, can be helped along by the use of a common rubric for all the papers.

Matching Beliefs and Practices in Assessment

12

MARK LEE

SCENARIO

Soraya Ramlawi is an experienced history and economics teacher who is concerned about how her assumptions about assessment practices influence what she does in the classroom. She uses informal practices during the course of her day to judge how her students' learning is progressing. She admits that informal assessments are conducted "on the run"; they are holistic and intuitive judgements that do not have explicit criteria. As well, she uses pen-and-paper tests to provide summative information about student learning. She combines the results of these scores with her intuitive judgement of student performance to arrive at student grades.

This year, as a better way of tracking qualitative changes in student learning throughout the year, two teachers in Soraya's school implemented a problem-based and student-centred curriculum, and they began assessing students' portfolios. While Soraya believes that problem-based instruction that is meant to promote growth in student learning should be used and assessed, she feels that accurate assessment of portfolios is quite difficult. Soraya knows that one obstacle to achieving this alignment is inconsistency between what she believes and what she does. She understands that summative test scores and her intuitive judgement are the two main sources of information that she uses for grading. But she does this despite her espoused belief that student achievement should be measured with clearly articulated indicators of student growth.

WHAT YOU WILL LEARN IN THIS ESSAY

- that identifying and documenting assessment practices helps to avoid negative consequences;
- that collaboration with colleagues is a useful method of identifying and documenting instruction and assessment practices;
- that the process begins with a description of assessment beliefs and favourite practice;

- that the process ends with a matching of these beliefs with practices, to identify a fit.

DISCUSSION

Soraya is a reflective individual who understands that the criteria she brings to making her formative judgements about student progress are unclear. She is troubled because she cannot clearly articulate how she integrates the holistic formative assessments that she uses to judge her students' progress with the results of pen-and-paper tests. While she trusts her intuitive judgements, she knows that her teacher training has influenced her teaching and assessment practices. For example, she is aware of her tendency to view knowledge as a quantitative accumulation of facts, and not (more correctly) as a set of integrated understandings that become more complex (qualitatively) as students learn. Soraya fully appreciates the school's reporting requirements, which emphasize counting learned facts and concepts and knows that this reinforces her tendency to assess students quantitatively.

Soraya begins her exploration by observing other teachers. Initially, she spends one period per week visiting Steve, her next-door neighbour. Steve is a history teacher who is implementing a problem-based curriculum and is creating and applying assessment rubrics to help him assess both the process and the quality of student learning. Soraya makes informal notes about Steve's instruction and assessment practices. After about two weeks, Soraya and Steve begin to discuss what she has noted. Soraya notices that, although there seems to be some inconsistency between Steve's instruction and his assessment practices, he has successfully assessed his students' portfolios and has created a rubric that identifies qualitative changes in student learning.

Steve explains that his favourite assessing tool is the ICE model, a continuum that begins with the Ideas level where pupils show evidence of having learned facts. The next level on the continuum is the Connections level, at which students demonstrate their ability to make connections within the curriculum or between the curriculum and aspects of their own lives. The highest level shown on the continuum is the Extensions level, at which students extend their connections in some original way.

Soraya notices, however, that while Steve espouses the need to assess qualitative changes in student learning, his instructional practices are consonant with a teacher-centred approach to teaching and learning. Steve says that he is concerned about "getting through the curriculum" and tends to spend a significant portion of his instructional time transmitting facts to the students. Steve's summative assessments show this; many of his test questions require that students recall facts and concepts, not show that they can make connections or demonstrate extensions. As well, Steve uses some student-centred activities and his rubric to assess qualitative change in student learning, but, overall, this seems to be an "add on" to his transmission-based forms of instruction and assessment.

Soraya notes that Steve is interested in, but somewhat uncomfortable about, her observations of his practice. She also sees that several conversations are required before Steve can talk about the inconsistencies that she sees.

During Soraya's final visit, Steve indicates that the conversations with Soraya have been helpful, that they have served as a catalyst for self-understanding. Steve explains that he has come to realize that it is his assumptions about the role of a teacher that partly explain the inconsistencies in his practice. He has traditionally viewed the teacher as the one who transmits knowledge. This assumption has hindered him in implementing a student-centred style of instruction, a style that could measure qualitative changes in student learning, such as portfolio assessment.

Soraya uses part of her planning period to visit Elaine's classroom as well. Elaine is a secondary teacher who is concerned about the appropriateness of her assessment practices. She is a committed educator, is extremely busy, and worries that her apparent lack of time for her own learning and reflection hinder her capacity to make changes in her teaching. Soraya notices that discussions with Elaine during the first few visits focus on defining Soraya's goals for visiting the classroom. Several visits take place before Elaine feels comfortable talking about her instruction and assessment practices. Even more visits take place before she is able to speak to Soraya about the rationales that underlie her practices.

Soraya comes to realize that instruction and assessment practices are rooted in personal values as well as in the various features of learning and assessment theory and practice that are discussed in teacher training courses and among colleagues. She jots down moments in her conversations with Elaine that seem significant. After a few weeks, Soraya reviews her notes and is surprised by the themes that emerge: Elaine's assessment practices seem to have changed somewhat since Soraya started observing Elaine's teaching. For example, early on, Elaine used a rubric that measured quantitative increases in student knowledge, not qualitative changes in student learning. Later, Soraya notices that Elaine has developed a new rubric and that she used it inconsistently. When Soraya asks about this, Elaine explains that, while she believes that formative assessments measures student growth, she feels that measuring quantitative learning "worked for her."

Soraya also notices that her discussions with Elaine are producing "aha!" moments, during which Elaine states that she has become aware of one or another assumption that has underpinned her thinking and behaviour. For example, Soraya points out Elaine's tendency to assess students individually and not use summative pen-and-paper tests in a group situation.

During one lunch-time conversation, Elaine declares, "You know, I didn't realize it before, but talking to you about this habit has made me realize that I am seeing the class in terms of individuals rather than as a collective. I guess this way of viewing the class makes the style of assessment I use more individual- than group-oriented."

Soraya's experiences in these two classrooms motivate her to look at a couple of journals that treat teacher learning and belief. She notes the results of her perusal:

- Beliefs or changes in beliefs do not directly influence teacher assessment practice in simple or predictable ways.
- Practice in and of itself does not simply influence teacher beliefs about assessment and learning.
- The relationship between teacher belief and practice is reflexive and complicated.
- A change in belief or knowledge does not necessarily result in a change in practice.

There are several factors that complicate the relationship among teacher belief, teacher knowledge, and teacher change: we need to be motivated to reflect upon what we are doing in order to make changes to what we do; habit is a powerful force that influences our ability to make changes or even consider what it is that we do; our assessment practices can become justified to us just because we have been doing these in a certain way over a long period of time.

It is useful for us to be aware of the influence of tacit (implicit) knowledge. We rely on concepts and knowledge in our everyday lives that we are only partially aware of. These exist in our minds as sets of deeply interrelated schema, which cannot help but influence how we understand teaching and learning. Before we can make meaningful changes to our practices, we need to become explicitly aware of the assumptions that underpin our instruction and assessment practices. Not doing so will surely result in our merely "adding on" new ideas and practices; we will not fundamentally change the way we do things.

One of the best ways that we can become more aware of what we do and why we do it is to have other professionals observe our instruction and assessment practices and offer their feedback. Collaboration with our colleagues can assist us in tapping the complex and deeply rooted features of knowledge that influences our thinking and practice. Discussions about our practice need to be repeated time and time again, as iteration helps us learn.

Soraya realizes that having a professional friend help her identify her assessment and instruction practices is a useful way for her to become aware of her underlying assumptions and then to help her make sustainable changes in her practice. The recent experience in her colleagues' classrooms has given her an intuitive sense of how to collaborate with a friend, but she feels a need to find a systematic way of doing it and wants to have a framework. These, she believes, will help her know whether her collaborative efforts are working.

A brief look through a couple of articles on action research and teacher-researcher collaboration gives her some ideas. The articles suggest several criteria for good collaborative relationships, which are crucial to fostering teacher learning. These include:

- The goals and roles of the collaborators must be made explicit and need to be compatible.
- Dialogue among professional collaborators must be repeated.
- Dialogue must be extensive and feature some form of narrative used by each collaborator.
- Other meaning-making mechanisms, such as non-verbal communication or other symbols (like drawing or role-playing), enhance the products of the collaborative process.
- Power hierarchies must be reduced and/or made explicit through role switching or the sharing of roles.
- Significant time must be allotted for successful collaboration.
- The roles and functions of the collaborators are expected to change as the collaboration evolves.
- Trust must be built throughout the collaboration.
- Contextual support (in the form of support from colleagues and administration) is useful to the success of collaboration.

Soraya feels that having another teacher offer feedback and critique her assessment and instructional practices might be intimidating and emotionally charged. She wants to examine, in an informal and ongoing way, the progress of her professional collaborative relationships. To do this, she builds a rubric that shows what improving collaborative processes and products could look like. This tool includes three categories: "beginning collaboration"; "intermediate collaboration"; and "advanced collaboration" (see Figure 19).

Feature of Collaboration	Beginning	Intermediate	Advanced
Dialogue	• Dialogue between collaborators is infrequent and of short duration. • Dialogue focusses on the negotiation of activities roles and goals. • Consensus on opinions is often an unstated goal.	• Dialogue between collaborators is frequent. • Dialogue has moved beyond a negotiation of roles and goals and is now focussed on attempts to make meaning. • Consensus is no longer a goal of the interaction.	• Dialogue between collaborators occurs frequently and is of sufficient duration that important issues are tabled and discussed. • Dialogue involves role switching, conflict, and features collaborators' understanding and articulation of personal assumptions.
Meaning-Making Mechanisms Other than Dialogue	• Only dialogue is formally used in the construction of meaning.	• Diagrams, pictures, or other symbols are occasionally used to communicate ideas to others.	• Non-verbal communication and symbols are are used to communicate ideas, feelings, and thoughts. There is evidence of meaning-making occurring within as well as between collaborators.
Power Hierarchies	• Significant differences in power and authority exist between collaborators that interfere with open dialogue. These hierarchies are not discussed or dealt with. Little trust is evident.	• Power hierarchies have been discussed openly. Their existence influences the scope and depth of dialogue. Trust is limited.	• Power imbalances have been dealt with strategically to minimize their influence on dialogue. Collaborators may openly discuss issues directly related to differences in power and authority. Trust is evident in the confidential nature of some of the information that passes between collaborators.

Time	• Small amounts of time are allotted for collaborative activities. Dialogue occurs in "the cracks of life," is hurried, and lacks focus.	• Separate units of time (i.e., after school) are allocated for lengthy periods of dialogue. Collaborative activities are planned to occur over extended periods (i.e., over a semester).	• Some spontaneous collaboration occurs as significant issues arise within and between collaborators. Time is allocated to these collaborative moments as a significant professional priority.
Contextual Support	• Collaboration is seen as a novelty or intrusion into the professional life of the school. Administration does not support time or other resource allocation for collaborative activity.	• Professional collaboration is tolerated within the school. Several teachers participate in this activity while others remain unengaged. Administration sees collaborative activity as an "add on" to professional development.	• A culture of professional reflective and collaborative activities is emerging within the school. Many staff participate in collaborative interactions with their peers that involve discussions and mutual observation of practice. Administration sees collaborative learning as a core feature of professional development and allocates resources, such as PD speakers, in direct response to themes and questions that emerge as collaborative products.

Figure 19. The three levels of collaborative processes

CONCLUSIONS

Soraya now feels that engaging in collaborative activities with a colleague and recording the results of her activities will provide her with a way to identify and document: her assessment and instruction practices as these are evident in her classroom; the types of explicit and implicit assumptions that underlie these practices; and the quality of the professional collaborative process that she experiences. She believes that this new understanding will help her to see more clearly the alignment that exists between the way she instructs and assesses. She feels that collaboration will give her clues that will help her make changes in her practice.

Creating Time and Space for Teachers to Improve their Practice

13

HELEN SNIDER

SCENARIO

Ann Haileyberry, a principal for sixteen years, returns to school from an all-day principals' cabinet meeting. She checks her in-box for urgent messages and then settles at her desk to review her notes from the meeting. Ann reflects on the lengthy to-do list from the day's meeting. She begins to plan discussions over the next few weeks with the teachers in her school to encourage them to take part in a whole-school plan that will focus on improving student learning and assessment.

Ann knows that her teachers already have heavy workloads. However, she also appreciates the research she studied in her graduate courses that suggests that principals and teachers share leadership and responsibility for student learning. She hopes to create a climate that will provide opportunities in which teachers can support and consult each other as they individually help improve their leadership skills and consequently improve the school's effectiveness (labelled "capacity-building" in the literature). But how can already over-worked teachers take on the additional task of formulating strategies for better learning and assessment? This is the dilemma she will discuss with her staff at next week's meeting.

WHAT YOU WILL LEARN IN THIS ESSAY

- why there is a need for teacher growth in conceptual understanding of educational reform;
- how changes in the workplace may lead to changes in teacher practices;
- how certain changes enhance teachers' conceptual understanding and promote professional inquiry;
- how building the capacity for organizational and cultural change within the school can refine the nature and craft of teaching;

- what specific supports are valued by classroom teachers to improve their skills in assessing students;
- what changes in school leadership are needed to bring about substantial changes in assessment of student growth in learning within schools.

DISCUSSION

A question frequently asked by teachers is, Why are so many changes in teacher practices necessary now? The question is often followed by the comment, Traditional teaching practices have served us well in the past.

One answer, of course, is that classroom teaching is a much more complex and sophisticated enterprise than it was twenty years ago. Traditionally, teachers were viewed by many as only semi-professionals because they spent a relatively short time training. Now, however, teachers are viewed as full professionals and as such deserve and require ongoing opportunities for professional growth. Classroom teachers have far more expertise than they previously did and should, accordingly, be given more opportunity for leadership within their schools, to participate in important decisions, and be allowed greater self-governance.

Nonetheless, many classroom teachers need help in shifting from the old patterns to the new, from being led to leading, from merely transmitting knowledge to students to helping them learn complex thinking and inquiry practices. These changes in the workplace require a common vision, a collective commitment, and full cooperation among all levels of staff and administration. In order to understand what is expected of them in a changed educational milieu, teachers need both time and a trusting environment that allows for questioning and personal exploration.

In recent years, creating the right environments for improvement at the school level has received a lot of attention in districts across the country. Expectations for both student and teacher performance that are embedded in a prescribed curriculum require a high degree of teacher collaboration to manage the numerous responsibilities inherent in a milieu of broad-based accountability.

What is needed to support these expectations? Teachers say that they need time and professional support to understand the role of daily and large-scale assessment as an integral component of the learning process (as opposed to assessment as a managerial requirement). "It was easier when all assessment was performed by the teacher and the main reason for it was the provision of report cards," says one of Ann's more experienced teachers. Now it is necessary to acquire and work with a new technical language and new skills.

It is a challenge to create an organizational culture that supports a new kind of learning community. Two essential ingredients that teachers need in order to refine assessment are time and space. Teachers need opportunities to grow and develop together in teams, working toward common goals.

As Ann noted, however, teachers already have full daily agendas. Thinking more systematically about their practices and how to teach so that their students can achieve maximum learning opportunities requires time and the opportunity to be part of learning communities, where they can have discussions with others in their field. Within these learning communities, teachers find themselves working less independently and more collaboratively on agreed-upon curriculum items that have a specific focus; they discuss what their students are expected to learn and how to improve their performance.

One way to start would be to have teachers collaborate with the goal of agreeing on important goals for student learning. The next step would be to start validating effective practices and improving upon less-than-effective uses of class time. In this scenario, the professional dialogue focusses on how best to improve student learning.

As well, in order to facilitate the development of professional learning communities, administrators need to pay attention to the quality of the structural and cultural conditions in schools. Optimum conditions, according to one group of experts in the field (Newmann, Secada, and Wehlage, 51-53), exhibit the following characteristics:

- a shared governance that increases teacher influence over school policy and practice;
- interdependent work structures (such as teaching teams), which encourage collaboration;
- staff development programs that enhance technical teaching skills consistent with school missions for high-quality learning;
- autonomy for schools to pursue a vision of high intellectual standards;
- increased opportunities for communication and trust;
- parental involvement in a broad range of school affairs.

In order to come up with the enabling factors that facilitate changes in both the workplace and teacher practice, all concerned need to ask: What is the purpose of our school? How well are our students learning and how do we know? What needs to change to achieve our common goals? Researchers have noted several changes as this process unfolds. As teachers begin to share assessment purposes and practices in more depth and with greater authority, the focus of their conversations begins to expand to include the well-being and character of the school as a whole. The conversation also begins to change as school improvement plans focus on specific areas for improvement and concentrate resources on specific goals, the dialogue among teachers becomes more focussed on use of class time, instructional practices, and improvement in student performance.

As school staffs become more involved in making substantive changes, the nature of staff meetings changes. The roles of principal and classroom teachers become more integrated and classroom teachers start articulating the school's vision and discussing how to design school improvement plans. Evidence of improvement occurs as:

- staff meetings become more than information sessions and include in-service components that connect assessment with instruction and learning;
- teachers share successful practices with each other and discuss why some practices are more or less successful than others;
- exemplars and rubrics provide bases for setting common standards for student performance;
- teachers are able to more readily state their commonly held understanding of standards for student performance.

A supportive and collaborative environment allows opportunities for teachers to share their expertise with colleagues in a dynamic problem-solving context that works across grades and across curricula. As teachers engage in this sharing process, some other changes occur that may not have been expected when the initial decision to collaborate was made. Teachers report that they experience less isolation, their sense of membership in the school community increases, and their professional satisfaction comes from measurable indicators that improvement in student learning is occurring.

In due course, as teachers refine their understanding of assessment purposes and design, they will choose assessment instruments that allow for a high degree of integration between instruction and instrument. Essentially, teachers themselves experience new learning—about classroom instruction and student learning, about their schools, about the process of change, and about themselves as professionals.

There are several ways that Ann herself can enhance her teachers' understanding of changes in educational process and thus promote changes in their assessment practices. For example, she can encourage teachers to state their needs for professional growth in, say, the use of rubrics, exemplars, and/or authentic performance tasks. The school can link each teacher's professional growth plans and performance evaluation to school improvement plans. Finally, she can provide teachers with opportunities to observe others' classrooms, attend workshops, meet with colleagues, and discuss school improvement initiatives in other schools.

More specifically, in Ann's school, improved teacher understanding of the design of assessment instruments, for example, led to changes in purpose and emphasis in classroom instruction. This development resulted in a more effective connection between assessment and learning. As well, in-service support for teachers to develop new instructional and assessment strategies resulted in more teachers increasing student responsibility for their own learning and self assessment. This refinement of understanding of assessment measures also resulted in increased support of teachers for assessment as an integral component of learning, program planning, and modification.

In the middle of this process, one of Ann's more experienced teachers asked, "Why do classroom instructional strategies continually need adjusting?" Ann provided some context:

> In the standards-based reform occurring throughout the country, ongoing data collection at the provincial level is used to monitor programs and improve instruction across a jurisdiction. Formative and summative assessments are interpreted and acted upon at the classroom, school, district, and provincial levels. Additional support to meet the needs of exceptional students in an effort to enable them to meet provincial expectations must be provided. And, besides, ongoing research in Canadian schools clearly shows that, when schools adopt a common focus and receive support using a research-based approach, along with partnering with parents, significant, even dramatic, improvement is evident.
>
> In this context, building capacity for new understandings of teaching becomes necessary. Capacity-building in a school begins with establishing a framework for creating initiatives that allow teachers to grow and develop together in the interests of improving student learning. There is no preconceived blueprint for capacity-building in schools. It is a creative, customized process, tailored to the needs of a particular school. The intent is to create effective teams that work toward teaching common goals. The process is incremental and requires commitment as teachers learn to be reflective and supportive of each other.

The notion that people should acquire additional qualifications over the course of their careers, that the organization has a responsibility to invest in the improvement of those qualifications, and that people should be expected to meet higher expectations for competence over the course of their careers is at the crux of the new notion of accountability and capacity-building. Little more than a decade ago, some school systems did not have the technical capacity to collect, analyze, and report data on schools. As evidence about performance of schools accumulates, successful schools are being examined to shed light on why some approaches seem to work and others don't. Teacher effectiveness and school culture is positively affected when schools build the capacity to utilize staff expertise and nurture consensus on school purposes and goals.

CONCLUSIONS

This essay has treated the notion of building capacity to achieve organizational and cultural change in schools. Several indicators will inform Ann of the emergence (or absence) of a "community of learners" within her school as she guides her staff to formulate strategies for effective assessment practices. She has made a checklist for herself and her staff:

- Have we created a trusting environment in which teachers can question and experiment with new approaches and strategies?
- Have we created teacher collegiality in meeting the academic program needs of all students within a school? (Is program development viewed as a continuum across the grades and subjects?)
- Have we created shared values and educational philosophy among our staff?
- Have we created opportunities for professional dialogue in staff/division/department meetings?
- Have we created shared responsibility for the success of all students in the school?
- Have we created utilization of teacher expertise in subject areas, school organization, the life of the school?
- Have we created opportunities for celebration of accomplishment among teachers and students?
- Have we created articulated support by the administration for teacher educational endeavours?
- Have we created teacher involvement in building a professional community within the school?
- Have we created recognition for work well done by teachers and students collectively?
- Have we created opportunities for parents to act as partners in reaching consensus on school issues?

Professional Learning for Individuals through School-Based Collaboration 14

LYN SHULHA

SCENARIO

During their first year of teaching, Cara and Gavin worked together to understand how modifying their assessment practices might better serve the special-needs students in their classes. Their efforts did not go unnoticed. This year, they have been invited to join the school's Assessment Committee, which traditionally coordinated professional activities for staff around a selected theme in assessment. Cara and Gavin look forward to having a voice in shaping the initiatives around this year's theme: assessing exceptional learners. They wonder how their learning experience last year might be expanded into meaningful learning for their colleagues as well. It is one thing to work with a friend, but how do you work with a whole staff?

WHAT YOU WILL LEARN IN THIS ESSAY

- that successful professional learning is triggered by a need;
- that teachers share certain characteristics that makes them potential collaborators;
- what systematic collaborative inquiry looks like in action;
- what creates the relationship between individual and joint learning;
- how you can identify a dilemma for investigation;
- what strategies are useful for pursuing new ideas to support teacher learning;
- what criteria exist for monitoring the quality of collaboration;
- what techniques can be used to encourage school-based professional development.

DISCUSSION

Collaboration Defined

In preparing for their first meeting as part of the Assessment Committee, Cara and Gavin revisit not only what they learned during their first year of teaching but also how they learned it. They talk about their work together as collaborators. For Gavin and Cara, this collaboration is a model of learning that has already had significant pay-offs.

By definition, collaboration is working in some equitable way with at least one other person on some task or dilemma. In an educational collaboration, the task is most often to gain a deeper understanding of some facet of teaching, learning, or schooling. For collaborators, action and learning are interdependent. The search for understanding leads to action; action, in turn, is the catalyst for both independent and joint learning. If the new learning is sufficient to at least temporarily resolve the dilemma, then the need for collaboration diminishes. If the new learning sharpens or alters the dilemma, even slightly, the search for understanding is likely to continue.

Last year it was their desire to gain a deeper understanding of how to assess the exceptional learners assigned to their classes that prompted Cara and Gavin to engage in reading, consulting with each other and colleagues, revising their assessments, and analyzing their students' responses to these revisions. Each effort they made to learn more about assessing exceptional learners allowed for new and more complex insights into their own practices. This in turn spurred them on to joint exploration.

This year, the Assessment Committee considers its options. As they always have done, they mount a one-day school-wide workshop that begins with a forty-five-minute keynote address offered by an expert. They follow this up by directing the staff to think about a standard task and report on it at the end of the day. Given the amount of work that Gavin and Cara have already done with the special education coordinator around this year's theme, the three of them are asked if they would take the lead in organizing the event.

After some discussion among themselves, the three come to the second meeting of the committee with a new proposal. They are willing to work closely with any staff member who has a specific interest in the assessment of exceptional learners. They will report back to the committee on both the number of teachers who show interest and the dilemmas that draw them together.

But what is a worthy dilemma? Gavin's major dilemma was Josh, a student whom Gavin taught every day and whom Gavin had misjudged. Josh's inability to succeed on Gavin's early tests was not from lack of effort on Josh's part, as Gavin had assumed. Gavin wondered how he had misjudged this student. He also wondered what else there was about Josh, and indeed the other learners in his class, that he might not understand. Gavin wanted his assessment practices to be fair for all his students, but he was no longer sure what "fair" meant.

Early in his collaboration with Cara, Gavin became aware that, as he learned about how to accommodate exceptional students, he also needed to be open to learning about himself as a teacher. In the beginning, it made him uncomfortable to think that his decisions about teaching and assessment might be negatively affecting his students' capacity to learn and achieve. As a new teacher, he needed to gain confidence, and pursuing this dilemma with Cara gave him that: both he and his students stood to gain from the inquiry. They decided to invite their colleagues to a meeting to be held the following Wednesday after school.

How Collaborators Connect

Cara and Gavin's original collaboration grew out of very modest and informal beginnings. While they knew little about each other initially, they were each willing to learn what the other thought was important about teaching and assessing exceptional learners. They began to trust each other, and this learning and trust led to mutual professional respect.

At first, collaborating was useful because it saved time. It allowed each of them to access more resources and ideas than they could muster on their own in a limited time. It was also an opportunity to work in a less isolating context. Wrestling with a dilemma within the confines of their own classrooms was less risky than collaborating, but it was also less motivating. As the two of them worked and learned together, their reasons for doing so changed. They discovered that their work was being fueled by a growing confidence in their ability to discuss the professional decisions they were making about the assessment of exceptional learners with colleagues, administrators, students, and parents. A rewarding spin-off was the growing sense that they were doing a better job of assessing students of all abilities.

Nineteen of the seventy-seven teachers on staff responded to the call to meet. Cara and Gavin opened the gathering by asking each member of the group to post one question about exceptional learners themselves and another about their own assessment practices. For an hour, the group discussed the common themes that emerged from these lists, paying special attention to distinguish between what they believe intuitively and understandings that can be supported with evidence. Gavin and Cara then told the story of their collaboration and its pay-offs and invited those who would be willing to commit to one semester of systematic inquiry into an aspect of assessing exceptional learners to come to a second meeting. Fifteen teachers returned for the second meeting.

Collaboration and Professional Learning

The depth of collaborators' participation influences the quality of their learning. Cara and Gavin realized that their own success the previous year was due, in part, to their willingness to make a commitment to regular meetings. Another reason was that they took action between meetings, such as gathering and examining resources independently or testing out an instrument.

Cara and Gavin also managed to build a significant degree of playfulness into their inquiry. While the nature of their work together was certainly serious, they allowed space to imagine, express, experiment, challenge, risk, visualize, reflect, and reconsider—all without serious consequence. And, as time went on, they felt comfortable blending social and professional activities. Working on a problem around lunch or coffee allowed them to understand each other better, and, with familiarity, it became easier to challenge each other's thinking and make suggestions for action.

The second meeting seemed to fly by. Cara and Gavin set up an exercise that helped members of the group connect with others who had similar interests. The group identified several specific dilemmas around assessment. Behavioural disabilities were of significant interest to several people, so two groups of three were established around this theme. (One group taught students who were primarily academically oriented; the other group was interested in how to help those who were in applied, or work-oriented, programs.) Another group of three shared an interest in integrating the assessment of learning skills as a regular part of their classroom activities (i.e. assessing how students organize information, manage time, show initiative, work independently, work in teams, and demonstrate effort). Two teachers from the English Department wanted to focus on how to help students with reading difficulties, and the remaining four teachers linked up because they each had students identified as "gifted/learning disabled." Each of these groups met independently to identify what their members would do to begin the inquiry process.

The coordinator of special education agreed to set up and monitor a web site with a chat room, meant to help the various groups post and receive feedback on their questions and the strategies they were testing out in their classrooms. Cara and Gavin remembered drawing on a wide variety of resources: policy documents, professional literature, research findings, and the understandings of students, parents, and experts in the field. They agreed to help all the groups locate the resources they needed and to make requests for support from the assessment team as the need arose. As a way of consolidating their progress as a large group they agreed to meet as a whole group once a month.

The quality of collaborative learning that results from this kind of teamwork is dependent, at least in part, on the quality of the resources introduced into the dialogue. The Internet, for example, may offer many ways to resolve a dilemma, but good judgement is necessary to assess accuracy and adequacy of the information there. At first, Gavin and Cara thought their task was to "find the answer" to their dilemma in a particular resource. The more they learned, however, the more they discovered that tools such as checklists, tracking sheets, and observation forms were most useful when they were accompanied by information that allowed them to consider their implications in their own teaching.

As important as motivation, commitment, playfulness, and good resources are, the heart of collaboration is the unique form of dialogue, sometimes referred to as a "purposeful dialectic." Purposeful dialectic serves two very specific purposes. The first is to help each individual in the collaboration make explicit the implicit knowledge that underpins many of the on-the-fly decisions he or she makes on a daily basis.

Tacit (implicit) knowledge is not the same as intuition. It is a set of highly integrated assumptions and understandings that gradually accrue with experience. It can be called "working knowledge" and is frequently contrasted to "theoretical knowledge." Cara and Gavin challenged each other to talk openly about why they were doing what they were doing, not only to better understand each other's values, ideas, and practices, but also to better understand their own.

The second goal of purposeful dialectic is to help reveal the contradictions and gaps in the reasoning used in decision-making. These gaps are very difficult to see when one is working alone. Cara reminded Gavin once that the only place he couldn't see in his classroom was the place where he was standing! It is when they describe beliefs and how these relate to practice that individuals reveal what may be readily apparent to others as incongruities.

For the purpose of identifying these gaps, Gavin and Cara didn't always accept what the other had to say. They did, however, make a concerted effort to respect the ideas that the other presented. They demonstrated this respect for each other by listening, clarifying and reframing ideas, offering alternative explanations, and introducing new ideas. These activities made it possible for each of them to hear their own assumptions, values, beliefs, and ideas through the voice of the other.

For Cara and Gavin, the purposeful dialectic meant subjecting their professional ideas and practices to tests of reasonableness based on what they were learning through their actions and discussions. Sometimes this meant having the utility of their approach confirmed; other times it meant restructuring their own notions of teaching and learning so that they were more congruent with notions of good practice emerging in the scholarly world. Gradually, Cara and Gavin became better able to identify contradictions in their own arguments and to create more powerful rationales for their actions.

Gavin and Cara asked that each group bring the resources they had used each month and be willing to talk about some practice or instrument that they had experimented with in the classroom. The special education coordinator arranged to have a specialist from another school or from the district office act as a reviewer.

Each small group took about fifteen minutes to present its work, but the response from the visiting colleague evoked a significant amount of discussion. What was intended to take an hour lasted almost two! Still, everyone agreed that it had been excellent use of those two hours. They pointed out that it had been some time since an organized professional-development activity had allowed them to:

- see some of the practical strategies that people were trying;
- examine how these new strategies were connected to what was known about exceptional learners, assessment, instruction, district policy, parents' needs;
- hear how these strategies were being received by students;
- discuss with each other and an "expert" the power of these ideas and how they might be adapted for their own contexts.

Collaboration is a unique form of professional learning. A fundamental assumption is that new approaches to any dilemma must be based on accurate information and sound reasoning. Gradually, with action, and through a purposeful dialectic, collaborators begin constructing joint meanings about both the complexity and appropriateness of responses to the dilemma. Joint meaning-making is an ongoing process, which involves a concerted mutual effort to synthesize a wide variety of learnings into a set of understandings that have merit, significance, and utility when applied to the dilemma.

The goal of collaborative effort is not to get everybody to do the same thing in the same way. Rather, it should be thought of as joint meaning-making that acknowledges the unique qualities that individuals bring to the dilemma and the even more unique nature of the classrooms in which learning has to be applied. For this reason, in joint meaning-making:

- the use of language is clarified, and variations in use, when justifiable, are honoured;
- the meaning attributed to any piece of information or behaviour must be defensible;
- when new learnings are applied, the resulting behaviours or consequences are open to examination;
- learning is traceable to some combination of individual and joint effort;
- all resolutions of the dilemma, even if they are temporary, reflect the best thinking of the collaborators at any given time.

The power of collaboration as a professional learning model lies in its fluidity. Collaborative groups can vary in size, in composition (members with similar roles or multiple roles), in points of interest, and in duration. For individual teachers, the opportunity for meaningful professional learning can be as close as a dilemma and a willing collaborator.

CONCLUSIONS

The first meeting of the Assessment Committee in second semester was scheduled to hear Cara, Gavin, and the special education coordinator report on the findings from the collaborative learning groups. Once again, the committee received a counter-proposal from the trio. Reporting on professional collaborative learning is a unique process. Findings ways to consolidate learning and express learning in a way that is meaningful to others often requires moving away from tradition notions of reporting. This essay has shown how one collaborative group tackled that challenge.

Note: For more about Cara and Gavin's experience with Josh, see Chapter 3.

Creating a Climate for Change in Assessment Practices

15

HELEN SNIDER

SCENARIO

Principal Ann Haileyberry recently received results from the annual provincial large-scale literacy assessment for Grade 10 students. She spent several hours studying the results and has met with her staff to distribute copies of the Provincial and School Literacy Report for their information and response. The assessment results and implications for planning next year's program will be the focus of the next staff meeting. Ann would like to see increased professional dialogue and teamwork among departments and across curricula to improve literacy, which has been a focus during the past few years. She wants to see concerted efforts from all the teachers in her school to provide students with a variety of advance organizers, study skills strategies, rubrics, and exemplars to help them succeed.

Her dilemmas are: how to develop a culture in her school that supports the premise that the results of assessment of student work (both ongoing-classroom assessment and large-scale assessment) can and should provide clear evidence that a teaching strategy or process has worked or not worked, and whether any programs need re-examination and adjustment.

Central to Ann's understanding of how to solve the dilemma is acceptance of the view that assessment provides feedback to guide teachers and students, informing them about what to do next and perhaps providing insight into how to do a better job. The analysis of assessment data as a key to school improvement requires an organizational structure within the school that acknowledges the importance of performance results in planning and modifying a program. This in turn requires acceptance of the idea that assessment results are an integral and ongoing component of the learning process. Many of her teachers, however, are not used to thinking this way and thus are opposed to external monitoring.

WHAT YOU WILL LEARN IN THIS ESSAY

- how organizational structure and culture affect learning environments in schools;
- how more productive learning environments can be fostered in schools;
- why there is a need for a professional collaborative community in schools;
- how a "technical" instructional culture contributes to effective classroom teaching and related assessment;
- how to develop a technical instructional culture in classroom instruction and assessment;
- how shared leadership can lead to improvement in student academic performance;
- what the changing-professional-teacher workplace looks like;
- how the structure and culture of a school affects its capacity to enhance student learning;
- how professional, more technical instructional environments in schools contribute to a clear focus on improvement in student academic performance and sound instructional and assessment practices;
- how broader, more inclusive school leadership helps achieve specific goals for improvement in student learning.

DISCUSSION

Schools as workplaces may be viewed as social organizations in which the climate and the performance of both students and teachers either facilitate or inhibit learning environments. Successful change in climate can happen only through an active, engaging process that involves administration, classroom teachers, students, parents, community agencies, and individuals. They all need to work together to respond to changing environments, draw lessons from past successes, detect and correct errors, and visualize and build images of a desirable future.

Ann was able to locate in the literature a number of indicators of an effective climate:

- Teachers collaborate with each other easily and eagerly.
- A school-wide focus on student learning is honoured by all.
- School goals and norms are clearly articulated and agreed to.

- Reflective dialogue and professional inquiry occur routinely.
- Classroom successes and uncertainties alike are shared.
- Teacher and organizational initiatives that promote shared leadership and individual professionalism are supported.
- The notion of parents as partners in the academic performance of students is clearly evident.

But how to get to this state was a challenge! Luckily, however, during her principals' courses, Ann had read much of the literature on change strategies. She took a look at her old notes to see which strategies might apply to her staff and school, and selected those points she thought might achieve a new emphasis on assessment and accountability:

- Have staff meetings that emphasize the identification of academic improvement to which specific action plans and timelines are attached.
- Promote lesson planning that connects objectives and expectations to teaching and assessment.
- Call collaborative team meetings that focus on sharing responsibility for success in the school for all students.
- Ask for clarification of expected student performance through the use of rubrics and diagnostic analysis of learning outcome.
- Encourage exploration of strategies for achieving targeted outcomes followed by detailed action plans to improve individual student achievement.
- Conduct data analyses of assessment results to modify program and provide direction in the planning process.
- Provide opportunities for parents to familiarize themselves with curricula and school programs; provide a forum for parents to seek clarification and discuss the program and their children's performances.
- Give feedback and celebrate successful procedures and strategies (i.e., that achieve academic goals).
- Share successful practices at school, district, and provincial levels.
- Encourage engagement in ongoing professional dialogue.

Ann found information in the literature indicating that schools that have refined their technical instructional cultures are more likely to show higher academic student performance than schools that have not. A technical instructional culture, as defined in the literature, insists on formal, precise language in instruction (e.g., the use of correct terminology and definitions, the scientific method, rubrics, and reliable diagnostic testing instruments). It encourages a focussed, detailed emphasis on intellectual dimensions of instruction and student performance.

How would Ann know when her school had attained such a climate? The indicators included:

- increased teamwork across grade levels and across curricula to develop and implement curricula and rubrics to assess student performance;
- recognition of, and reliance on, the expertise of the teacher in curriculum development, implementation, and program modification;
- the use of specialized technical, formal, or scientific language in instruction in various disciplines;
- the use of rubrics and levels of performance as guideposts to empower students in the learning process and self-assessment;
- the integration of assessment with classroom instruction by connecting expectations to outcomes;
- professional development opportunities for teachers to develop acumen in assessment and data analysis;
- increased use of long-range planning that includes assessment components;
- the ongoing use of achievement results in program planning and modification;
- increased teacher and parent understanding of assessment as part of the learning process.

Ann believed that her school already showed leadership in its attempts to change. Many of the teachers in her school had become experts in understanding how children relate to curricula according to grade level and how individual children respond differently to the same teaching strategies. These teachers had become especially knowledgeable about the needs and difficulties of struggling students. They had shown leadership by sharing strategies and resources to improve student performance with each other and with parents.

Ann realized that she had already done many things to involve her staff and school community in a model that refined individual skills and developed expertise school-wide. She had delegated leadership responsibilities among teachers, students, and parents whenever possible without diminishing their other responsibilities. When teachers improved their expertise in curriculum, Ann encouraged their taking on school and/or district leadership roles. This meant that she had to provide time and space for her teachers to do so. It meant that she had to coordinate the school's organizational structure to allow teachers to work together on such tasks as scheduling and timetabling, planning professional development opportunities, and planning for school improvement.

Marcia Nixon is one teacher who blossomed within this supportive environment. See Figure 20 for an example of the kind of daily planner that Marcia uses. And here are excerpts from her daybook notes:

> It all started when I was feeling very overwhelmed and confused by the level-system of reporting. I wondered how I could make my assessment as accurate as possible to reflect the numerous curriculum expectations. In addition, I needed something that was tangible and yet easy to maintain. To get a holistic picture of a student, I have come to realize that I need a variety of teaching assessment tools. These tools should be measurable and thus enable me to easily comment on the student report card. This organizational approach has helped me to manage curriculum expectations, assessment, and daily planning more satisfactorily.
>
> To begin with, I need a hard copy of the subject expectations from the various subject curriculum outlines. Next, I need dividers per subject and per strand in the subject field (e.g., in math, I would have a total of five dividers for each of the five strands—numeration, probability, measurement, geometry, and patterning. In language, three dividers are needed for three strands—reading, writing, oral/visual communication). I need to organize a divider (e.g., labelled numeration) together with a photocopy of two sheets of the expectation outline, and a class list for record-keeping organized by strands. I need to proceed in similar fashion with the other dividers for each curriculum expectation sheet and a class list.
>
> I then prepare my daybook using my standard daily planner. I create a master sheet on computer so that, on a day-to-day basis, strands are simply highlighted with a marker, as are resources used. I only need to add specific expectations, planned activities, and assessment tools each day.
>
> When planning lessons, I refer to Ministry expectations from the curriculum guideline sheets in my divider. This helps me to stay focussed on curriculum expectations that need to be addressed. Evaluation for a specific lesson is recorded on the student list under the appropriate strand.
>
> The following ideas for developing high-level thinking skills with measurable tools are working for me:

1. Date:

Subject: Mathematics

Strand: **Numeration Probability Patterning Measurement Geometry**

Resources:

Interactions 6	Manual pp.	Student Textbook pp.
Ontario Math Workbook	Manual pp.	Student Textbook pp.
Math Connections	Manual pp.	Student Textbook pp.
Math Quest	Manual pp.	Student Textbook pp.
Other		

Expectations:

Student Activity: (Sample)

Assessment (Sample Rubric)

****

2. Date:

Subject: Language

Strand: **Reading Writing Oral/Visual Communications**

Resources:

Nelson Spelling Language 6	Manual pp.	Student Text pp.
Nelson Reading	Manual pp.	Student Text pp.
Other		

Expectations:

Student Activity: (Sample)

Assessment:

****

Figure 20. Sample daily planner entries for Grade 6 mathematics and language

- I provide students with model samples of student work from previous years. I draw to students' attention the specific expectations that I am looking for, such as the detail on the title page. With each successive assignment I add or identify more specific expectations.
- I use book reviews from published texts as exemplars. Students substitute familiar novel titles.
- I use examples from literature (e.g., limericks from Edward Lear).
- I use visuals (e.g., Venn diagrams and charts) as strategies in teaching literature. Initially, these are done cooperatively, then in a group, then with a partner, and then individually.
- I use detailed and specific rubrics and highlighters to indicate student performance per category. Students can then see what they need to do to proceed to the next level of achievement.
- I use Ministry exemplars that illustrate Level 1, 2, 3, or 4. I arrange them on the blackboard and cooperatively discuss with the class how each exemplar is assessed.
- I organize group activities. I appoint a leader and discuss his or her role in making sure each member has an opportunity to contribute one item to the discussion and then open up the issue to group discussion. An appointed secretary records the discussion. A manager distributes and collects materials used. Group work is assessed initially by a teacher-created rubric. The class may proceed to a group evaluation rubric and sometimes a self-evaluation rubric.

CONCLUSIONS

One of Principal Haileyberry's main goals is to help her staff understand that assessment, far from being simply the teacher's summary judgement, is a process of systematically gathering information from a variety of sources and providing students with descriptive feedback for improvement.

With her collaborative approach to effecting change, Ann and her staff are working toward delivering programs and evaluation practices that ensure that all students are making measurable progress. Students and teachers alike are taking increased ownership of responsibility for learning. Students are being equipped with strategies for improvement in performance, resulting in more positive self-concepts. Teachers are engaging in increasingly effective classroom instructional and assessment practices. As an administrator, Ann's main task is to provide a climate that allows professionalism to flourish among her staff.

III External Assessments

A major dilemma for teachers is the reality of external assessments, usually created and administered by authorities outside the school and often outside the district. Many teachers find these assessments artificial and don't take the whole individual into account when reporting on the results. Nevertheless, these assessments are seen as useful markers for governments and administrators, because they provide data that help them decide where to allocate resources and when to update curricula. A major advantage of these assessments is that they are impersonal. They provide an objective look at student learning.

Unfortunately, some local authorities believe that the techniques adopted for these external assessments should be the norm for classroom assessment as well. Some educators (and parents and the general public) believe that teachers should not only emulate these assessments in their own classroom practices but also translate the results into "improved" student learning.

The three essays in this section look at the reality of external assessments from different classroom perspectives. The first essay examines how a teacher might validly use what the results say about student learning. The second looks at how teachers and schools can prepare their students to take these assessment tests. The final chapter delineates how a school district can legitimately translate the text results into improved student learning.

Balancing Criterion- and Self-Referenced Assessments

16

ROBERT PETRICK

SCENARIO

After a few years of undertaking large-scale assessments in her classroom, and the subsequent changes that trailed along behind the published results, Robin Peters, an elementary classroom teacher, begins to have serious doubts about her own philosophy about classroom assessment practices. In spite of the sometimes disappointing and confusing results she receives from these external assessments, she knows she could not have worked harder or more creatively with her students, and she considers her assessment approach both thorough and global.

Robin's principal tries to reassure her that any large-scale assessment is meant to provide only a snapshot of literacy and mathematical skills, but they both know what comes next: the school improvement plan, the studies, and the media coverage aimed at school-shopping parents. "How," Robin asks, "can I buy into the prescribed process of school improvement and still maintain a compassionate, individualized approach to learning, [and maintain] an assessment scheme that complements that approach?"

WHAT YOU WILL LEARN IN THIS ESSAY

- that two approaches to assessment—criterion-referenced and self-referenced—can be combined effectively;
- that each approach has both strengths and weaknesses;
- that some assessment tools accomplish both purposes;
- that support groups can be a source of ideas for new approaches;
- that involving the stakeholders can be helpful in using assessment techniques.

Criterion-Referenced Assessment	Self-Referenced Assessment
• standards-based • students must reach a fixed bar of achievement on a common product • "next-steps" process	• individualized, growth-oriented • differing styles of products to be expected

Figure 21. A comparison of criterion-referenced and self-referenced assessment

DISCUSSION

Two differing approaches to assessment are currently in use. The first is "criterion-referenced," which identifies whether or not a student has achieved some curricular expectations. Failure to do so will result in the teacher identifying reasonable steps to help the student achieve those expectations. The onus of implementing these steps is on the teacher. The second is "self-referenced," which is associated with the term "growth." It employs observable components that are linked to learning or teaching opportunities that have immediate benefit to the student. The student will integrate the learned component into the fabric of his or her learning within the whole curriculum or make a novel extension that will serve as an anchor for new growth in some learning area. (See Figure 21 for a comparison of the two approaches.)

Each of these two approaches has a set of primary stakeholders, that is, those who are most likely to receive immediate pay-offs. The primary stakeholders of criterion-referenced approaches are the teacher, the administrators, and the parents. The teacher uses information gathered to make effective use of time and to be accountable to parents. School administrators use information gathered to develop action plans to address deficits in student performance across the school. Parents are comfortable with the kinds of assessment that describe their children's shortcomings because they are in a position to react directly and try out suggested mitigating strategies. It is, after all, the way they were taught as children.

Stakeholders in the learning/teaching approach can best be identified as partnerships, if certain conditions are met. First, there is the student/teacher unit, which will benefit from such mechanisms as routines that allow data to be recorded and used in a format useful for learning and teaching. Second, there is the student/parent unit, which can benefit from this type of assessment as long as there is an opportunity and protocol for effective communication between student and parent. Then, naturally following, is the student/teacher/parent partnership. The word naturally is key here. Robin has found in her previous teaching experience that if she builds in something that is comfortable and easy to understand, parents will collaborate eagerly and willingly.

Limitations of Each Approach

Each of the two approaches has limitations, that is, inherent characteristics that restrict its use. In Robin's experience, the criterion-referenced tools cannot paint a picture of the whole child at a particular moment. Any teacher is, nonetheless, anxious to understand criterion-referenced data in the context of the child whom he or she has gradually come to know. Robin's experience is probably much the same as that of other teachers. They try to make a broad meaning of the results of these tools, taking into account their rounded view of each child. Robin doubts that this approach promotes a sense of ownership or accountability to self. In the eyes of students who are routinely described as below standard, the rubric, or scale, approach that often accompanies the criterion-referenced approach tends to be an impediment to growth.

Too, inherent in this approach is the difficulty of accounting for affective factors in student learning, such as motivation and interest. Nor does it offer a convincing way of explaining discrepancies in performance from day to day. Typically, the tools associated with this approach require a large amount of student work to help the teacher decide where a student can be placed reliably and what the next steps might be. Any student can provide better work on one day than on another. The likely causes of such deviations are changes in motivation or interest, or perhaps other, more specific, personal events. These are not easily picked up by the one-shot assessment tool.

Using an ongoing, self-referenced approach to assessment, on the other hand, can be unwieldy and vague in its application. Consider the situation in which a student may have many teachers. It may be up to the home-room teacher to collate information and present an uncomplicated picture of the student to the parents. It would take a prodigious logistical effort on the part of all staff to put aside their individual assumptions in order to arrive at practical remedial strategies that could be used for the benefit of the student. And, in order to work, this approach needs precise rules. Without logical and sensible parameters, the process tends to result in vague and therefore meaningless conclusions about students' growth. See Figure 22 for a summary of the shortcomings of each approach (if adopted exclusively).

Finding a Balanced Approach to Assessment through Collaboration

To make a combination of two assessment approaches work, Robin found that she needed support. Luckily, she was able to find collaborators of like mind among various levels of teaching (elementary, secondary, and university): "It really helps to find some sympathetic colleagues who will help shed

Criterion-Referenced Assessment	Self-Referenced/Teaching Assessment
• limits ability to describe the "whole" student	• can be unstructured
• learner has difficulty producing ownership of learning	• difficult to implement (particularly when classes are on a rotary system)
• does not account for affective learning factors (motivation and interest)	• identifying "next steps" requires much thought

Figure 22. Shortcomings of criterion-referenced and self-referenced assessment approaches

light on what you feel about assessment. Meet regularly, compare notes, do research, and back up each other's ideas."

As Ann continues to function as a member of her collaborative group, it becomes clear that all members agree on one overriding value: a serious consideration of growth is a necessary component in any assessment, not only for the recognition of growth but also to allow growth to happen. Robin explains:

> It is within this atmosphere that I have been able to continue engaging in some of my favourite teaching practices, discussing with colleagues their value and appropriateness in the context of existing policy. I have found often (not always) that, with some reworking, these time-tested learning opportunities will either fill in gaps left by the criterion-referenced approach or, in fact, work side by side to complement it. Here's how this sense of balance works for me.
>
> In making decisions either to keep or abandon my traditionally favourite projects and procedures, I have established an informal weeding process as I undergo the planning phase of creating my program each year. A case in point is my love of creating a musical production at some point during the year. I have always been convinced that children need to have this experience every year, not just once per age division (primary, junior, and middle school). Heretofore, I have never been faced with having to justify its value in educational terms. But, in the wake of the school improvement phenomenon, the first part of the process of decision-making is now a considered justification for creating a musical every year.
>
> When I have convinced others (and myself) that the musical can be integrated thematically into the provincial curriculum and that it explores the outcomes prescribed in curriculum documents (however loosely), I proceed to the next step. This step involves injecting into the assessment picture a component that allows for the evaluative judgements of the student.

The developmental model of self-reference that Robin describes encourages students to revise, modify, and reflect critically upon the processes of learning. This is accomplished in part through the "invisible" guidance of the teacher and through a variety of self-evaluative opportunities such as assignments or extended activities that result in significant written products. These opportunities, along with other self-assessment formats, will keep the tasks fresh in the minds of students.

Robin has found that the teacher must address self-assessment systematically if it is to be effective, including a faithful adherence to a routine of feedback to students, self-evaluative comments. This takes time, but it is the private, personal type of message that a student will closely examine and take to heart. "Do not make the mistake of overloading the student with cumbersome, comprehensive self-checking lists at the beginning of the school year," Robin maintains. "The student is just developing an understanding of where you are headed. Keep it simple, and build on what each child demonstrates as a need." After working with this kind of self-assessment for a while, the teacher will likely want to retool other events in his or her repertoire, such as school trips, invention conventions, subject fairs, school councils, and chess tournaments.

Teaching and assessment methods that lead to higher levels of learning do result in better retention. With this in mind, teachers can think of goal-setting as a useful formative measure to promote both student control over learning and accountability. Here are examples of points that teachers might present to their students:

- When working and playing at school, I feel most confident in these areas … (e.g., spelling, playing sports)
- I think I need to become more confident at … (e.g., solving math problems, making new friends)
- Here are some new skills I'd like to master this year … (e.g., learn volleyball, make a musical instrument)
- These are ways I can help other students at our school this year, so that our school can become a better place to work and play ... (e.g., get a reading buddy, try out for school council)

Robin finds that the goals she established in the autumn need to be revised periodically. She advises: "Schedule times for revision [of goals], or they tend not to take place. Parents should also be involved in the process of goal-setting. A useful storage space for the statement of goals is the portfolio of work exemplars established for each pupil. The portfolio is readily accessible to the student, teacher, and parents."

Robin has her students write an essay in June, which acts as a summative evaluation of the year's achievement. She finds emphasis on reflection a practical and gratifying activity. Robin provides the following possibilities for her students to consider as starters for their first drafts:

- things I accomplished;
- things I didn't quite accomplish;
- new things or skills I learned;
- my favourite moments connected to school;
- an overall statement about how I grew as a person and as a student.

CONCLUSIONS

In an atmosphere of constant change and shifts in paradigms, it is prudent and helpful for educators to keep all assessment options open. One way to ensure a comfort level among them is to find a group of colleagues to work with. The interest and support of a group of like-minded people will go a long way to help teachers feel more secure in navigating their ways through the potential minefields inherent in large-scale assessment.

Preparing Students for External Assessments

17

CINDE LOCK

SCENARIO

Susan Turnbull has been teaching Grade 3 students for twenty years. She gets a sense of her students and their abilities during the first week of school and, by the end of the first few months, she knows their strengths and weaknesses and is comfortable informing parents about their children's progress.

Last year, her students were required to write a provincial assessment in mathematics, reading, and writing. While Susan views these tests as an interruption in her teaching time, she supports their introduction because she wants to see if her own assessments coincide with those at an external, objective test. She also wants to learn about how her students compare with those in other schools and other districts.

Last year, Susan was concerned about how to prepare her students for the provincial assessment without cheating. She worried that, because teachers had different ways of preparing their students, the results wouldn't be very fair. She also worried that any pressure the administrators at her school applied on her to make sure that her students did well might negatively influence her teaching practice. Susan is trying to make the best of the situation and at the same time determined to find the most appropriate way to prepare her students for the assessment. She wants to draw anything positive she can from the experience. Her dilemma is: How can I be helpful and positive with my students without distorting the value of the tests?

WHAT YOU WILL LEARN IN THIS ESSAY

- what the purposes and value, benefits and drawbacks, of large-scale assessments are;
- how various examples of test preparation activities relate to accuracy of test scores;
- what is meant by "test-score pollution";

- how large-scale assessments may legitimately influence teaching practice.

DISCUSSION

Susan decides she needs to go on a mission of research and understanding. Her first stop is at the web site of the testing office. She is surprised to discover that not only is the web site easy to find, but it is also filled with useful information. It has a hotline number for questions, sample assessment units, advice about how to become involved, and much more. But she isn't interested in this right now; she will come back to it later. First, she wants to know what the testing office sees as the purpose and potential value of their assessments. Aha, here it is! She reads it aloud from the web site: "Our mission is to ensure public accountability and to contribute to the improvement of education for all learners."

All the words surrounding this mission statement are positive: "We value the well-being of learners"; "We promote constructive improvement"; and "We involve teachers in all aspects of our assessment programs." This is not quite what Susan thought she would find. The large-scale standardized assessment tests had been received very negatively at her school last year, and she had lost a great deal of classroom teaching time because of them. But maybe there is something positive for her to draw from this new mandate.

Susan clicks on the section entitled "How to Prepare Your Students for the Tests." There is a large set of files to download that provide examples of test questions, sample assessment units, and information about the outline and construction of the assessments. While these might prove useful to her in preparing this year's group of students for the provincial assessment, Susan knows that her colleagues everywhere are engaging in numerous other activities to prepare their students. Are these activities acceptable, appropriate, expected, or common across schools?

She talks with three colleagues, two from her own school and one from a neighbouring elementary school, and prepares a list of the types of activities they are using to prepare students for the tests. They include:

- teaching test-taking strategies such as deciding which types of questions to answer first, interpreting instructions, and identifying instructions that might be common to all tests;
- discussing time-management skills for answering test questions;
- providing students with questions similar to those on the previous year's tests that they can take home and practise with their parents or guardians;

- conducting a mock test the week before the real test;
- restructuring teaching practices throughout the year to align them with the content tested and with the style and format of the testing;
- helping students improve their written communication skills.

Susan thinks that her students would clearly be at a disadvantage if she decided not to adjust her teaching in some way to help prepare them for the standardized test. It is comforting for Susan to hear that all three of her friends are anxious about which activities are appropriate and which are not. She asks herself, "If this list is varied and represents only views from three teachers, what would the list look like if, say, three thousand teachers were questioned? How different are assessment preparation strategies from classroom to classroom?"

In the discussions with her colleagues, Susan finds that policies about exemptions and absenteeism seem to differ between the two schools. The teachers at Susan's own school exempt only those students who clearly would be frustrated and humiliated by participating in the testing. This exclusion amounts to about 5 percent of the students in Grade 3. The other schools exempt as many students as they can—almost 19 percent of the Grade 3 students. They believe that standardized testing is a negative experience for students in general and that the more students exempted, the better. As well, the teachers at this school encourage low-achieving students to stay home from school on the days when the test is being administered.

How can anyone compare results from school to school, or even within one school from year to year, when assessment and preparation practices vary so greatly? Susan wonders how valuable it will be to even try to interpret the student results when they come in. She decides to do some more reading. She remembers a recent article in a professional journal she regularly receives. She looks it up and finds that teachers have done everything from providing cookies and pizza as motivators to giving hints or answers during the test. The author of the article noted that there is a term for all of these activities (that is, the ethical/unethical and appropriate/inappropriate activities): "test-score pollution."

The term "pollution" is used because these inappropriate practices serve to contaminate achievement variables with non-achievement variables. The author also noted that these inappropriate activities directly affect the reliability of the test scores and thus make it difficult to compare test results from one teacher to another or from one school to another. Susan feels an overwhelming need to discuss this issue with the other teachers at her school so that they can decide together what activities to use to prepare their students for the standardized assessment tests. Consistency seems to be the keyword.

As Susan reads further, she finds that the author lists some typical negative influences that large-scale assessments have had on teaching practices. She writes some of these down to discuss with her primary team: "teaching to the test; narrowing the curriculum; decontextualizing; emphasizing low-level cognitive activities."

Susan is not surprised to find that teachers are, in effect, "teaching to the test" when they are helping their students succeed on standardized tests. Isn't that what she herself has been struggling with? But what she is surprised to learn is that the overall influence of teaching to the test is that teachers tend to teach only what is tested, especially as it becomes more and more important that students' results improve. The curriculum thus becomes "narrow"; expectations that are not reflected on the test end up not being taught at all. It is easier to test one thing at a time (deconstructing) and bits and pieces of the curriculum out of context (decontextualizing), and teachers tend to match these in their teaching. Because complex thinking is hard to test, ultimately teachers tend to emphasize low-level thinking skills.

This is a very negative view of testing. "Surely," thinks Susan, "there must be something of value in all this large-scale assessment stuff." She returns to the testing agency's web site, where she had found the words so reassuring and the perception of large-scale assessment so positive.

Susan is pleased to find that there is indeed something included about how the testing office intends to meet its second mandate, which is "to contribute to the improvement of education for all learners." She learns that, apparently, it all has to do with the style of testing that is being implemented. She knows that performance-based assessment is the type of testing that is mandated for her province. And most of the reading she has done about the negative influences of testing point to multiple-choice and selected-response-type tests. Performance-based tests are free of many of these faults.

The intention of using the performance-based style of assessment is that tests can be constructed to include context-based questions that combine curriculum expectations and require students to truly engage and use complex thinking skills in the creation of their solutions. Susan is sceptical about this explanation. Maybe this type of testing won't result in the same negative influences on teaching that she just read about, but what will the influences of this type of testing be on practice? Susan decides to record over the course of this year all of the practices she engages in with her students in an effort to prepare them for the testing. She also decides to record those activities she doesn't have her students participate in because of time limitations related to the testing or preparation for it.

CONCLUSIONS

While Susan is eager to understand how standardized assessment testing might influence her teaching practice, she is also determined to make it as positive an experience as possible for the learning and well-being of her students. She is going to make it work for her as well, and have the most positive experience possible as a result. She makes a point of asking the teachers in the lunch room the next day to relay only the positive experiences they have had with regard to the introduction of large-scale assessment in their school. She discovers:

- One teacher volunteered to participate in the scoring of the assessment last year and discovered that it was the most rewarding professional development experience she has had to date; she connected with other teachers in other schools and other districts, discussed key curriculum issues in depth, and felt that a world of possibilities and resources had just been opened up for her.
- Another teacher decided that, if she had to participate in standardized testing, she would ensure that the results be put to good use; she joined the School Improvement Planning Team and was actively engaged in using these, and other, school data to make decisions related to the improvement of numeracy and literacy skills for students in the school.
- A third teacher talked about how receipt of these data reminded him of the importance of regularly reflecting on his practice; it was a point in time when he gained perspective about the big picture of teaching; maybe there were issues about the depth to which the results could be analyzed, but he knew his students well; what he didn't do often enough was look at the overall achievement of the individuals in his class and the group as a whole to see where he needed to put more emphasis.

Susan now has a new mission—to be mindful of the potential of standardized testing to negatively affect her teaching while at the same time to derive everything positive from the experience for both herself and her students.

How Successful Districts Utilize External Results

18

DON KLINGER

SCENARIO

As district administrators, Louise Sampson and Frank Liscombe are responsible for the implementation and support of district-wide initiatives to monitor and improve student achievement. Assessment results from the Ministry of Education have indicated that 30 percent of the Grade 9 students in the district have failed to meet the expected standard in mathematics and science. Louise and Frank reported these results to school administrators, and the responses ranged from disbelief and despair to complete agreement. Many of the principals used the discussion to describe how the assessments were an unfair measure of student achievement in mathematics and science.

Louise and Frank have been assigned the task of developing a district initiative to improve student achievement in mathematics and science. However, the district mathematics and science teachers' association has advised Frank and Louise that there is little evidence that there is a problem with math and science achievement in the district, and that the evidence that does exist is of little value in implementing policies for improvement. Their concerns are about the lack of depth in the reporting of the Ministry examinations. As they are leaving a lengthy meeting with the teachers, Frank confides in Louise: "There is a lot more to this task than I expected!"

WHAT YOU WILL LEARN IN THIS ESSAY

- from a district perspective, what the forms and purposes of large-scale assessments are;
- what the critical issues in interpreting and reporting large-scale assessment results are;
- how standard-setting procedures can be developed to examine acceptable levels of performance;
- how stakeholder groups can be provided a role;

- how assessment results can be used to examine achievement and support district initiatives.

DISCUSSION

Responding to Large-Scale Assessments

Successful school districts are those that use assessment information to identify overall strengths and weaknesses within the district and then do something with that information. But Louise and Frank are not interested in using the information to identify and sanction specific schools or personnel. Rather, they plan to use the information to set direction and support professional development and training for teachers, administrators, and even parents at the district level.

Louise and Frank's district uses achievement results from external assessments administered by the Ministry of Education (the provincial level), but there are additional sources from which such information is derived, for example, a larger jurisdiction (e.g., a country or a group of countries) or a smaller jurisdiction (e.g., a school district). Unlike external assessments (e.g., the provincial or federal level), assessments at the district level provide an opportunity to design an assessment that arises from a perceived or identified need. This information is not limited to measures of academic achievement. Districts can collect other relevant information, including (but not limited to) the percentage of students obtaining specific letter grades, average marks, graduation and/or promotion rates, award winners, course selection, citizenship, or attendance, as well as information about stability and trends.

Large-scale assessments can have many stated purposes. Increasingly, this information is being used for system accountability or to support and implement district initiatives for maintaining or increasing student success. The stated purposes of the assessment dictate the design, structure, and information that can be obtained. From a district perspective, assessment information is used to monitor overall achievement of students at various points in time and if possible in relation to external references. If the external references are other students, schools, or districts, the assessment information is considered to be norm-referenced. If the reference is an external and independent standard of achievement, the assessment information is considered to be criterion-referenced.

Soon after their meeting with the mathematics and science teachers' association, Louise and Frank began planning the next steps in the process. Frank noted how angry the teachers in the association were about the process. One particular teacher stated, "After teaching in the district for twenty years, I do not need an external government exam to tell me that the students are struggling in math more than ever before." Louise then mentioned a conversation she had with a neighbour in which he said how impressed he was by his children's education. He stated, "My children are able to deal with mathematical concepts and solve problems that I remember first seeing in university."

These seemingly disparate views about student learning reminded Louise and Frank that the process and findings of large-scale assessments will inevitably be viewed differently by different groups, depending on what they perceive to be at stake. These stakeholding groups include teachers, administrators, parents, community members, and, of course, students. Louise and Frank concluded that any new initiative that did not take into account the perspectives of these various groups would likely be dismissed immediately by them. And it would make discussions richer if they included the stakeholders in any discussions leading to initiatives.

When they went looking for direction, Louise and Frank found that others, too, had found ways to involve stakeholders in the process. For example, in many jurisdictions, parent councils were part of the school planning committees. Frank read a copy of the 1994 report published by the General Accounting Office of the United States (Cheliminsky and York). The report noted that the British Columbia and Alberta Grade 12 testing programs had a high degree of teacher support. Their conclusions indicated that the inclusion of teachers in the development and marking procedures, as well as the good fit between teacher expectations and examination content, was the reason for the high degree of teacher support. Successful districts encourage their staff to become involved with such external examination programs.

Louise and Frank used this model to encourage teachers in the district to apply to work with the Ministry of Education as item writers, exam markers, or members of the standard-setting panels. Thus, the district has input into the format and structure of the assessment. And teachers become increasing aware of the assessment procedures; if the process is viewed by teachers as being sound and rational, they gain confidence in using the results.

Teachers in jurisdictions other than Frank and Louise's had reported that working with the large-scale assessments provided opportunities for professional development. Teachers and staff were able to share their experience with other staff and, most importantly, use it to help students in their learning.

With this as background, Louise and Frank then created their task force of eight stakeholders: teachers (including the one who made the comment at the meeting), administrators, and parents. Together they took on the

	Does Not Meet Expectations	Meets Expectations	Exceeds Expectations
District	30%	60%	10%
Provincial	28%	60%	12%

Figure 23. District results compared to provincial results

challenge of reviewing the assessment findings and developing appropriate recommendations in response to the results.

Strengths and Limitations of External Large-Scale Assessments

Teachers often distrust the results of assessments administered from outside. They often express the view that the tests do not reflect what goes on in classrooms, occur at the wrong time of the year, and do not provide specific results. The information gathered may provide broad statements about student achievement or about other background measures but does little to provide guidance. In contrast, assessment programs initiated within a district can easily involve district staff in the development and implementation of the assessments.

When the task force met for the first time, Louise and Frank started with the quote from the angry teacher, which they had heard earlier, at their meeting with the mathematics and science teachers' association: "After teaching in the district for twenty years I do not need an external government exam to tell me that the students are struggling in math more than ever before." And they then gave each of the task force members a copy of the results received by the district (see Figure 23 for a comparison of district results and provincial results).

Louise and Frank knew that they would face scepticism about the assessment results and the assessment program itself. They also knew that the results were often misinterpreted. Rather than avoid the issues, Louise and Frank offered the following precautions:

- Acknowledge and understand the inherent error in measurement and classification in the scores or proportions.
- Avoid interpreting the results in comparison to others (e.g., other districts or the entire population
- Acknowledge and understand the standard setting methods used to create the levels of achievement and subsequent categorization of student responses.

Although error information is generally reported along with the results, most people concentrate on just the scores themselves. Frank and Louise had witnessed some poor decisions that were based solely on scores. (These teachers hadn't taken into account the fact that the size of the measurement error increases as the number of scores decreases.) Most measurement error is found at the student- and class- or school-level, and the least amount of error is found at the provincial level. Hence, the task force was asked to consider the likely range of values that were incorporated with the reported values and the effect of this error on the subsequent interpretation.

While convenient, comparative data are always misleading, especially since different districts have different contextual factors. These contextual factors include, but are not limited to, neighbourhood demographics (socio-economic status, transience, family backgrounds), and location (rural, suburban, or urban). Louise and Frank asked the task force to consider whether the results shown in Figure 23 would be valid: (1) in a district with a high level of parental education; (2) in an affluent urban setting; and (3) in a district where the majority of students tended to go to university. The task force thought that such a community, with its generous resources and its general positive attitude to education might have higher standards in mind for their students. As Frank concluded, in some communities achievement at school is seen as the most important responsibility a child takes on. In other communities, however, students must balance achievement at school with jobs and family responsibilities.

Louise and Frank asked the teachers, parents, and administrators on the task force to give their own descriptions of the district and its students. The ensuing discussion, in which the participants considered demographic and contextual information provided by participants, some information obtained from district records, and the published assessment scores themselves, were the basis for the district profile.

It is one thing to balance the information provided by large-scale assessments and interpret the results cautiously (considering the precautions listed above), but the next step in the process, because of its complexity, is quite another. "Standard setting" is the general term used to identify the methods used to relate test results to characteristics of student performance and levels (categories) of achievement. While there are several standard setting procedures, they all require a judgemental process that establishes the range of student performance associated with each level of achievement. This information is then used to develop a description of expected student performance associated with each category.

Louise and Frank sent each member home with a set of completed student assessments. In preparation for the next meeting, the members were

	Does Not Meet Expectations	Meets Expectations	Exceeds Expectations
Expected Proportions	15%	65%	20%
Actual Proportions	30%	60%	10%

Figure 24. Task-force predictions compared to official results

asked to use their previous discussion to classify each of the samples into one of three categories: "Does not meet expectations"; "Meets expectations"; and "Exceeds expectations."

At the beginning of the next meeting, the members compared their rankings of the student work. They had little difficulty ranking the samples in terms of quality; however, there was lots of discussion about the classification that each sample should be given. This dilemma was the one that Louise and Frank hoped would occur. The members spent the first half of the evening discussing the skills, concepts, and abilities that students should be able to demonstrate at their particular level of their education. When the members were shown the official classifications of the students' tests, they were surprised to find how close they were.

The members were now ready for the next step in the process. Each member was asked to use their discussion and the district contextual information (both assets and liabilities) to estimate the proportion of students from their own district that they would expect to see in each of the categories.

As with the previous steps, there were differences of opinion. Interestingly, the teachers tended to have higher expectations for student achievement than did the other stakeholders. Throughout this meeting, Louise and Frank challenged the task force to determine a set of percentages that would be acceptable to each of the members (see Figure 24).

Frank then wrote the obtained proportions below. A comparison of predicted and actual proportions indicated that there was a higher than expected proportion of students in the lowest category of achievement and a lower proportion of students in the highest category of achievement. Further, these proportions were different even when the measurement error was considered.

One of the parents remarked, "It appears we have work to do at both the low and high ends." Several of the members of the task force asked for more information, for example, about the proportion of males and females in each group, which might be a very important factor. But, though there were differences between the scores of males and females, the differences were not significant (see Figure 25). Differences existed at the school level too, but none of the individual school results were significantly different from the expected proportions predicted by the task force.

	Does Not Meet Expectations	Meets Expectations	Exceeds Expectations
Males	28%	61%	11%
Females	32%	59%	9%

Figure 25. A comparison of male and female students who did not meet, who did meet, and who exceeded expectations in official large-scale assessment results

Using Large-Scale Assessment Results to Develop District Initiatives

Increasingly, the broad conclusions drawn from large-scale assessment results are being used to support and implement district goals and initiatives for maintaining or increasing student achievement, and Louise and Frank decided to do just this. They realized, as did the members of the task force, that the current method of reporting the assessment results could be used only to identify general areas of strengths or weaknesses, that is, provide guidelines only.

More and more, such large-scale assessment programs provide either item- or "strand"-level information, which can be used to highlight specific strengths and weaknesses. Within some assessment programs, a separate summary is generated that highlights specific areas, of weaknesses and strengths, that appear in the data. Louise and Frank wanted to find out if this type of information could be obtained for the district; such information would greatly help the task force in their job. When they contacted the Ministry of Education, they were informed that such information was not available at that time. However, the officials did agree to meet with Frank and Louise at some future date to discuss the type of information that they might be able to provide.

Generally, district assessment results provide a structure with which to begin discussion, but it is only through subsequent and more detailed analyses that specific information can be generated. And, while general information might provide broad statements about achievement (or other measures of schooling in relation to a particular standard or population), it does little to provide guidelines. Nor can general information provide data that can be easily used by teachers to modify instruction. Rather, broad general conclusions can provide a mechanism to begin to develop goals and initiatives. Successful districts acknowledge the strengths and weaknesses of such data.

Although the Ministry of Education was not able to provide specific information, the task force was able to work with the sample papers to identify difficulties and weaknesses in the students' achievements. The task force used the information from the sample papers and the teaching experience of those within the task force to identify the relevant skills and concepts that students were lacking or consistently found difficult.

The final meeting was devoted to preparing their report, which outlined the role of and procedures used by the task force, and its findings. Louise and Frank wanted to present the report in a timely and thoughtful manner. Hence, they organized meetings with each of the stakeholder groups to discuss the findings. Task force members were involved in these meetings, and they were careful to present both the positive and negative findings. Armed with their new understanding of the large-scale assessment as developed by the task force, Louise and Frank were now ready to proceed with their own job of introducing a model for the implementation and support of district-wide initiatives to improve student achievement.

Based on the findings and conclusions of the task force, each of the schools in the district was asked to develop a plan that would focus on increasing the math and science achievement of low-achieving students while also increasing the number of students demonstrating high levels of math achievement. School-based teams developed plans that were appropriate for their own school. In many jurisdictions, districts and schools are expected to show measured improvement over a short period of time, often over the next assessment cycle. Recognizing that such short-term plans would not help to build successful initiatives, Frank and Louise developed a model in which the plans were to be implemented and monitored over a minimum of three years.

At the same time, district resources and funds were allocated over the same three-year period to sponsor district-wide professional development programs. Rather than support periodic after-school workshops, these funds were used to sponsor annual district math and science conferences and week-long retreats that would provide teachers with an opportunity to investigate alternative ways to teach math and science.

CONCLUSIONS

Louise Sampson and Frank Liscombe work for a successful school district. Its success is not based on the current academic achievement of their students, although one day it might. Rather, it is based on a commitment to support educational initiatives while not ignoring information or attaching blame to individuals. The response to the official results of a large-scale assessment was to work with stakeholders to examine the content of the test and develop a method to determine not only the adequacy of this content but also the levels of success that students should be able to demonstrate. Ultimately, the discussions and conclusions do not focus on the assessment results but, rather, on the relevant skills and concepts that the test measures. Subsequent initiatives focussed on finding ways to help district personnel address those skills and/or concepts deemed to require attention. The success of this district is due to:

- its focus on student achievement, success, and growth;
- mechanisms that allow stakeholders to freely express their views and opinions;
- teacher and staff participation in district programs and procedures;
- the use of assessment results to guide policies and initiatives;
- the use of assessment results to support rather than judge or compare;
- policies and initiatives that reflect sound interpretations of results;
- acknowledgement of the strengths and weakness of assessment results;
- an understanding of large-scale assessment procedures;
- stakeholder involvement in the assessment analyses and subsequent initiatives;
- district expenditures that support initial and ongoing initiatives;
- a method of monitoring the success of school and district initiatives.

As the school year was coming to a close, Louise received a phone call from the teacher who had challenged Frank and Louise at their initial meeting. This teacher was calling to tell Louise that the teachers at the school had been busy modifying their math program and that three of the teachers, including herself, would be participating in a week-long math teachers' conference and retreat in the summer sponsored by the school district.

Contributors

JOHN O. ANDERSON works and publishes in the broad field of assessment but concentrates on teachers' assessment practices and large-scale assessment. He is a professor in the Department of Educational Psychology and Leadership Studies at the University of Victoria.

CHRISTOPHER DELUCA recently completed his Bachelor of Education degree at Queen's University. As part of his program, he created a professional portfolio on the complexity of assessing exceptional learners. Many of the resources and ideas included in his essay, including those suggested by the special education coordinator and those on the sample test, came from his portfolio.

DON KLINGER is a former high school teacher and district coordinator of assessment and evaluation for the Langley School District in British Columbia. He is a professor in assessment and evaluation at the Faculty of Education at Queen's University. His research interests include the examination of psychometric and policy issues of large-scale assessments, standard setting, and measures of school effectiveness.

MARK LEE taught high school history in Egypt before starting graduate work at Queen's University. He is now interested in international and cross-cultural evaluation studies as well as evaluation policy and classroom assessment. He is an assistant professor at Trent University in Peterborough, Ontario.

CINDE LOCK taught high school science and mathematics in Ontario, Egypt, and West Africa before becoming a self-employed program evaluator and researcher. Most recently, she has acted as coordinator of quality assurance for the Ottawa-Carleton District School Board. In this position, Cinde facilitated professional development to teachers in the area of assessment and evaluation and provided guidance to administrators in relation to school and district improvement planning.

TIMOTHY MOSSER teaches Grades 1 and 2 students in Belleville, Ontario. He has a Master's degree from Queen's University and has worked with prospective teachers on professional development portfolios. He is especially interested in involving parents in their children's education.

DAVID NOTMAN taught high school business and law for thirty years. He pioneered the use of cooperative education, portfolio assessment, and student conferencing at the high school level. He is the author of several business texts, has worked as a consultant for the Ministry of Education in Ontario, and has taught courses in assessment to prospective teachers at Queen's University.

ROBERT PETRICK is an elementary school teacher in Kingston, Ontario. Over a span of thirty years, he has taught children from a variety of backgrounds, including Ojibway, Cree, and Mohawk. His urban teaching experiences in inner-city and working-class neighbourhoods in Toronto and Kingston have motivated him to complete a Master's degree. The focus of this work is on the role parents and families play in the education of children.

LYN SHULHA began her career as a high school teacher and department head in northern Ontario. Since joining the Faculty of Education at Queen's University in 1992, she has taught courses in curriculum design, program evaluation, and classroom assessment. Her research in assessment and evaluation is predominantly school-based and collaborative, with an emphasis on individual and organizational learning. She is one of two Canadian representatives on the Joint Committee on Evaluation Standards based in the United States.

HELEN SNIDER has extensive teaching and administrative experience in Ontario elementary and secondary schools as well as in a Canadian International school overseas. She has a Doctor of Education degree from Boston University. Her research concerns what makes certain schools use assessment data well and others not. She is involved in teacher preparation programs in the United States.

ROBERT J. WILSON has taught at all levels in the educational system, from elementary students in British Columbia to graduate students at Queen's University in Ontario. He is interested in teachers' assessment practices and what makes these practices effective in enhancing learning.

SUE FOSTATY YOUNG began her career as a special-education teacher, working with profoundly developmentally handicapped children. Wanting to share what she had learned in the classroom, Sue moved on to teaching at the college level, where she developed an interest in adult learning theories, instructional development, and learning assessment. In addition to her studies, she facilitates courses in instructional methods, group dynamics, and reflective practice. Sue is a Doctoral student in the Faculty of Education at Queen's University.

—

Works Cited

Cheliminsky, E., and R.L. York. *Educational Testing: The Canadian Experience with Standards, Examinations, and Assessments.* General Accounting Office Report PEMD-93-11, Gaithersburg, MD, 1994.

Friend, M., W.D. Bursuck, and N.L. Hutchinson. *Including Exceptional Students: A Practical Guide for Classroom Teachers*. Scarborough, ON: Allyn and Bacon Canada, 1998.

Hutchinson, N.L. *Inclusion of Exceptional Learners in Canadian Schools: A Practical Handbook for Teachers*. Toronto, ON: Prentice Hall, 2002.

Newmann, F.M., W.G. Secada, and G.G. Wehlage. *Successful School Restructuring: A Report to the Public and Educators by the Center on Organization and Restructuring of Schools.* Madison, WI: Wisconsin Center for Education Research, 1995.

Ontario Ministry of Education [OME]. *Special Education: A Guide for Educators.* Toronto, ON: Queen's Printer for Ontario, 2000.

_____ . *The Ontario Curriculum: Grades 1 to 12,* Achievement Charts. Toronto, ON: Queen's Printer for Ontario, 2004.

Young, S. Fostaty, and R.J. Wilson. *Assessment and Learning: The ICE Approach*. Winnipeg, MB: Portage and Main Press, 2000.

Further Reading

Alberta Learning. *Unlocking Potential: Key Components of Programming for Students with Learning Disabilities.* Edmonton, AB: Learning and Teaching Resources Branch, 2005.

Barth, R.S."Teacher Leader." *Phi Delta Kappan* (February 2001): 443-449, 2001.

Biggs, J.B., and K.F. Collis. *Evaluating the Quality of Learning: The SOLO Taxonomy.* New York: Academic Press, 1982.

Black, P. *Testing: Friend or Foe? Theory and Practice of Assessment and Testing.* London: Falmer Press, 1988.

British Columbia Ministry of Education. Sp*ecial Education Services: A Manual of Policies, Procedures and Guidelines.* < http://www.bced.gov.bc.ca/specialed/ >, 2005.

Browder, D.M., F. Spooner, R. Algozzine, L. Ahlgrim-Delzell, C. Flowers, and M. Karvonen. "What We Know and Need to Know about Alternative Assessment." *Exceptional Children* 1.70: 45-61, 2003.

Earl, L.M. *Assessment as Learning: Using Classroom Assessment to Maximize Student Learning.* Thousand Oaks, CA: Corwin Press, 2003.

Elias, M.J. "The Connection between Social-Emotional Learning and Learning Disabilities: Implications for Intervention." *Learning Disability Quarterly* 27.1 (Winter): 53-63, 2004.

Elmore, R.F. *Building a New Structure for School Leadership.* Washington, DC: The Albert Shanker Institute, 2000.

Lovitt, T.C., and S. Cushing "Parents of Youth with Disabilities: Their Perceptions of School Programs." *Remedial and Special Education* 20.3: 134-142, 1999.

Perkins, D., and C. Unger, eds. *Teaching and Learning for Understanding.* Mahwah, NJ: Lawrence Erlbaum, 2000.

Schmoker, M. *Results: The Key to Continuous School Improvement.* Alexandria, VA: Association for Supervision and Curriculum Development, 1996.

Shulha, L., and R.J. Wilson. "Collaborative Mixed-Method Research." In A. Tashakkori and C. Teddlie, eds. *Handbook of Mixed Methodology*, 639-670. Newbury Park, CA: Sage Publications, 2003.

Shulha, L.M. "Evaluative Inquiry in University/School Professional Learning Partnerships." In V.J. Caracelli and Preskill, eds. *The Expanding Scope of Evaluation Use: New Directions for Evaluation*, vol. 88, 39-54. San Francisco, CA: Jossey-Bas, 2000.

Snider, H.J. "Reform through Assessment in Ontario Schools." PhD dissertation. Boston University. Boston, MA, 2001.

Specht, J. "Educating Exceptional Children: Current Issues for Educators." *Education Canada* 44.1: 4-7, 2004.

The Joint Committee on Standards for Educational Evaluation. *The Student Evaluation Standards.* Thousand Oaks, CA: Corwin Press, 2003.

Trehearne, M. *Closing the Literacy Gap: A Whole-School Approach to Prevention and Intervention.* Calgary, AB: Calgary Board of Education. February, 2002.

Wiggins, G. *Assessing Student Performance.* San Francisco, CA: Jossey-Bass, 1993.